brilliant

marketing

What the best marketers know, do and say

Richard Hall

PEARSON
Prentice Hall

Harlow, England • London • New York • Boston • San Francisco • Toronto • Sydney • Singapore • Hong Kong
Tokyo • Seoul • Taipei • New Delhi • Cape Town • Madrid • Mexico City • Amsterdam • Munich • Paris • Milan

PEARSON EDUCATION

Edinburgh Gate
Harlow CM20 2JE
Tel: +44 (0)1279 623623
Fax: +44 (0)1279 431059

Web site: www.pearsoned.co.

First published in Great Brita

© Pearson Education Limited

ISBN: 978–0–273–72123–9

British Library Cataloguing-in-Publication Data
A catalogue record for this book is available from the British Library

Library of Congress Cataloging-in-Publication Data
Hall, Richard, 1944-
    Brilliant marketing : what the best marketers know, do, and say / Richard
Hall. -- 1st ed.
        p. cm.
    ISBN 978-0-273-72123-9 (pbk.)
    1. Marketing. 2. Success in business. 3. Success--Psychological aspects. I.
Title.
    HF5415.H1855 2009
    658.8--dc22
                            2009011398

10 9 8 7 6 5 4 3 2 1
13 12 11 10 09

Typeset in 10/14pt Plantin by 3
Printed and bound in Great Britain by Henry Ling Ltd, at the Dorset Press,
Dorchester, Dorset

The publisher's policy is to use paper manufactured from sustainable forests.

Praise for *Brilliant Marketing*

Sharp, insightful and highly amusing ... so entertaining, you don't realise how much you're learning. * * * * * 5 stars!
Ian George, Managing Director of 20th Century Fox Film Company Limited

Richard Hall's book doesn't lie. It is brilliant! Read this book. It is stimulating, entertaining and nutrient rich. Written in an engaging and inspiring style, it is packed with ideas and examples and is a must for grads and seasoned marketers alike.
Tom Hings, Director, Brand Marketing, Royal Mail

Brilliant Marketing reflects all I know of Richard: not only is he a man of great humour and wisdom, but his belief in the endless possibilities of people's potential shines through.

Use this book to challenge yourself and the 'right way of doing things' – Richard will show you that the only barriers to success are lack of self-belief and passion for your brand.
Rupert Maitland-Titterton, Head of Public Affairs, Nestlé UK Ltd

I'm a huge fan of both Richard's writing and wisdom. This book is packed with brilliant nuggets that offer the kind of insight that will transform your understanding of the marketing mix and allow you to harness its potency. A must-read for anyone about to engage with this industry.
Rachel Bell, founder, Shine Communication

Brilliant Marketing is the antithesis of many a marketing textbook. Hall backs up his claims that the business of marketing should be a rollercoaster, with a high speed tour of what makes this profession great
Will Arnold-Baker, Managing Director, Publicis Ltd

Contents

Marketing has never been more important because business has never been so competitive.

Learn how to do it, where and why it's changing, how to be knowledgeable about developments and what drives change.

Most of all understand the customer and their new found powers.

December 2008 (what a time to try and write an upbeat book).

Author's acknowledgements

The challenge of writing a book on so broad a subject is considerable, but when it's about what you've spent your life doing it's rather like appearing on *Strictly Come Dancing* when you thought you were a talented hoofer, only to discover that you have two left feet.

Sam Jackson, my commissioning editor, has been rigorous in helping me keep on track. She is exhausted. My wife Kate has been utterly brilliant in making me focus. She is totally exhausted. I am surrounded by marketing warriors and heroes and heroines who've inspired me. From Richard French to Bruce Purgavie to Nick Horswell to Ian George to Rachel Bell to David Abbott to Sir John Hegarty and many others.

I hope this book helps young marketers do a better or even a brilliant job. It is designed to make them think and give them a basic toolkit. It is a springboard or, perhaps, a space-hopper to project them into a brilliant career.

There has never been a better time to be in marketing. And, do you know, I really believe this right now.

Who am I?

I spent my early career at Reckitts, RHM, Corgi Toys (Mettoy) before going into the louche and lovely world of advertising at French Gold Abbott, FCO (where I had the best time in my life until now) and finally at Euro RSCG.

I now run my own consultancy, chair a few companies, work for a charity, live in Brighton and watch with amazement at the firework display that is the economy of today.

I love the discipline and the art of marketing. I hope this helps its cause.

www.richardhall.biz

http: //marketing-creativity-leadership.blogspot.com

Publisher's acknowledgements

We are grateful to the following for permission to reproduce copyright material:

Chapter 4, overview of the Nike story adapted from *Nike Culture*, by Robert Goldman and Stephen Papson, SAGE Publications (©Goldman, R. and Papson, S. 1998) is reproduced by permission of SAGE Publications, London, Los Angeles, New Delhi and Singapore; Chapter 5, extract from 'The Strange Death of Modern Advertising' from *Financial Times*, 22 June 2006 with permission from Lord Maurice Saatchi and the Financial Times; Chapter 11, extract from 'New Shop Promises Results Clients Can Gauge' from *The New York Times*, 28 August 2007.

Every effort has been made by the publisher to obtain permission from the appropriate source to reproduce material which appears in this book. In some instances we may have been unable to trace the owners of copyright material and would appreciate any information that would enable us to do so.

Preface

What is this brilliant marketing thing?

Marketing is about the art of seduction. The art of making someone do something they didn't think they wanted to do, but found that in fact they did, once you'd persuaded them to try it, and now they want to do it again and again. Seduction is about making people want you, and so is marketing.

You can't seduce someone if they don't know you exist; if you don't engage with them and if they don't appreciate that you might have something going for you. So there's real technical stuff you have to get right. You don't just rush up to people as Graham Norton might, squealing 'Hallo, it's me!!'

Marketing is also fun. It's fun because when it really works you really know it – sales go up, share goes up, research tells you that it's working, you get write-ups in marketing magazines and there's a buzz about. But it's also fun because it's all about what makes people tick and human beings are the most fun that you get in life, so studying them as a profession is extremely pleasing.

The function of marketing has recently, again, been put squarely at the centre of the commercial stage as everyone has realised that the chase for sales, growth or, perhaps more realistically, survival is something brilliant marketers who really understand their trade customers and their end consumers can achieve but few others can.

I believe that you have to be brilliant at this stuff to make a real difference. Anything less than A* is a fail.

Let's assume you may already know a little about marketing or at any rate have a strong sense you'd like to do it. Although let's be a bit more ambitious than merely wanting to 'do it'.

So welcome to the strong, strong alcohol of brilliant-marketing: the fuel that really transforms things. And let's start by looking at some great stories to get ourselves excited about just how enthralling marketing has been for others and could be for us.

Marketing stories – gather round

 **example**

Nike. Just do it. Like FCO did it.

Virtually everything that Nike does has the mark of brilliance. When Nike was being launched in the UK in the 1980s, two posters stood out. One was the Wimbledon tennis shoes worn by McEnroe. Young John was at his 'man-you-cannot-be-serious' worst during Wimbledon, and the poster simply had a picture of the shoe and the line 'McEnroe swears by them.' The other was a running shoe used by marathon runners around the time of the London Marathon, when Ken Livingstone was trying to make his mark as the Mayor of London the first time round. His fame had also been enhanced by a brilliant pro-Ken poster campaign by Boase Massimi Pollitt. This was again a picture of the shoe, just that, no embellishments, and the line 'Dear Ken, here's the way to run London.'

How do you do brilliant things like this? You think about what the brand stands for and what the product does and then you tell it like it is.

 **example**

Happy cows. Great ice cream.

The launch of Ben & Jerry's ice cream (now owned by Walls, a division of Unilever). It had great PR – we all knew that it was owned, and that the various tastes were created, by the eponymous couple of rebels with long beards, both with hippy attitudes and both lovers of organic food. The product design was fun and exciting and not corporate in feel. The philosophy was encapsulated by an advertisement on the London Underground which proclaimed 'Mission statement: To make nice ice cream.' What more can you say? How great to ridicule 'mission statements'. And they are still having fun with the brand, declaring on their web site their adherence to 'peace, love and ice cream' and in their crusade to create a 'caring dairy, milking happy cows not the planet'. Rock on!

I love logos that make me smile

There are two great logos that make me feel funny every time I see them. Apple, a six-coloured, striped apple with a computer-generated bite out of it (twentieth and twenty-first-century Garden of Eden), it looks so perfect and such fun. And there's Google, again colourful but also three-dimensional, and through Dennis Hwang's Google Doodles it is contemporary too. The 'doodles' are the inventive way he plays with the logo on special anniversaries so you have the sense that the brand is constantly being refreshed. Both logos are meant for brilliantly self-confident, alive brands – no dead hand of corporate bureaucracy here.

So are you too busy to try and be brilliant at marketing?

Many people seem to feel too busy to even try and be brilliant nowadays. When a deadline is more important than the quality of what is done by that deadline we may have a few challenges to face. Despite the improvements in technology we have less time than ever. All executives are on 24/7/365 – BlackBerrys, iPhones, pagers. You can even call people on planes. (Hurray – no more opportunities to escape with soothing glasses of claret and a good novel – indeed they'll have video-conferencing on planes next – imagine the six-hour video-conference on route to New York – that's terrific. No, I don't think so.)

We have to find time to be more creative if we want to shine in marketing. This is not just a skillset thing, it's a mindset thing too. We have to find ways of maximising the stimuli to creative brilliance.

This book is a manifesto for brilliance – not new-wave brilliance but brilliance that comes from the kind of intuitive leap that all brilliant marketers make in working out how to get their target consumers to do and think something they otherwise wouldn't have thought about or done. Brilliant marketing is that magic stuff, the ideas, the actions and the campaigns that make a real difference.

Learn how to do it and have enormous satisfaction and fun.

PART 1

Let's get marketing into context – psychology, history and alchemy

CHAPTER 1

Introduction to marketing brilliance

Why it's been written

This book seeks to introduce you to the challenges and excitement of marketing. Having spent most of my life doing senior marketing jobs at three big companies, holding leading roles in three major advertising agencies and, more recently, advising a number of companies, both big and small, I have learned quite a few lessons in how to make a difference. I'd like to pass these on and help you see just why and how marketing is so important.

This changing world

The world in which we now live seems likely to be much tougher than the heady days of the early and mid-noughties. The rules are changing. Getting a sale is going to be much harder. And you know that times are tougher when marketing guys like me talk about sales more than they talk about image. But tough as it is doesn't mean it's impossible, just that we all have to work harder and smarter. And here are the three things that have leapt to the top of any marketing agenda:

i)   the quality of our relationship with our customers

ii) the value for money of our products or services and the recognition that we live in a dynamically priced world – price is the new variable

iii) the ability we have to reach existing and potential customers with good news; in uncertain times the radar systems out there keep on blanking off. Do not dare to assume you are still on your customers' screens.

brilliant tip

Marketing is – or must be – if nothing else, exciting. The process of persuasion has never been dull, but today we have a whole new set of tools available which means we can communicate better, proving nothing is impossible.

Other advice from long experience

- **The templates you find in most marketing text books don't work.** They are not bad books but they assume 'fit for purpose' is good enough. They make you ordinary and liable to create the cardinal fault of being boring. They are at best prosaic, and at worst career impeding.

- **What I learned from the best.** This book borrows from the experience and talent of the best and the best they have to say. David Abbott, Tim Bell, John Hegarty, Bill Bernbach, Rachel Bell and Ian George are more recent apogees. Most of all this. Marketing has more to do with art than science. More to do with feelings than logic. Which means this is not simply a 'how to do' book but a 'how to think about how to do' book. Mindset first; skillset second; smartset next.

> marketing has more to do with feelings than logic

- **Brilliance requires a little irreverence.** The assumption that accepted wisdom is good enough goes out of the window when the wheels fall off, and it's fascinating to see marketing giants like P&G and Nestlé do clever, small things like the latter's launch of Skinny Cow Hot Chocolate drink – showcasing the brand in Oxford Street and Manchester, at House of Fraser boutiques and at tasting sessions at George at Asda (which is heading to be and probably, by now, is the biggest UK clothes retailer). Focus on your core market and be there as they first encounter your brand.

● **Your curiosity is king**. Unless you are rushing around with boundless enthusiastic energy reading papers, looking at magazines, visiting shops, talking to bright people, you are missing out on the 'Semtex' of marketing breakthrough. In my world the eyes and ears have it and the mouth comes third.

● **Left brain: right brain**. Get them in balance but do not spend your life living on the left where no brilliant marketers live or ever have lived. Don't think too big, don't think too small, don't think too much. Just focus

> focus on trying to understand your customer

on trying to understand your customer. My best work was intuitive, but driven through with detail and remorseless execution.

The process of marketing

The process can be reduced pretty well to the following:

1 **Writing the brief** – the discipline of setting out what you have, what makes it special and what you need to get done. Do not fight shy of saying what you feel and think as well as what you know. This is your map.

2 **Defining your resources** – whom you have on your team, how much time and talent they have. Be clear about what they and you are capable of delivering. Next, how much

money do you have to spend? This will determine what you can and cannot do. Never bite off more than you can chew. To embark on a project that is overly ambitious is very foolish.

3 **Examining your options** – you have a lot of options. So long as you have a clear brief, then

focus on what you are trying to achieve

those that most economically and effectively match the objectives you have set should be shortlisted. One word is key here. Focus. Focus on what you are trying to achieve.

4 **Writing a clear and detailed plan** – the brief is your map; the plan is your itinerary. We go into this in much more detail later on. No one should ever spend a penny of a marketing budget without having a good robust plan.

5 **Executing the plan** – interestingly Harvard Business School are now saying it is execution that is more important than strategy. They have dozens of case studies where the strategy was fine and the execution was wanting. This is checklist time. Is everything ready on time? Is everything right? Is everything fitting together? Does the plan feel as though it's going in the right direction?

6 **Measuring the results** – everything you do needs to have an effect. Your job is to measure these. Are sales going up? Is share going up? Are people talking about the campaign? Is there any research to show how awareness, attitude or behaviour is changing? As a result of your review does anything need changing? Go back to the brief and make sure it still holds water. Never, ever keep pouring good money after bad.

This book helps guide you through this process. Whether you are a marketing executive or a brand manager in a middle sized or big company or doing your own marketing in your own company, the basic principles that lead to professional and brilliant marketing are the same.

Contained here are guides to the skills you need, the attitudes of mind that will help, knowledge of how the components of marketing actually work, examples of great and not so great marketing, the dynamics of marketing and the relationships you will need to build.

Marketing is a big subject, so if I sometimes seem to have galloped through a section and have left you a little breathless I apologise. Nonetheless, you'll find most of the things you need to get started on a brilliant marketing career or, if you are already on your way, here's how to lift your game and move to the next level. None of us is too old to learn and there's a lot of learning in here.

Making brilliance a benchmark

I believe you can make the journey from apprentice to brilliant marketer but it takes time and effort. Marketing is not easy. It calls for a lot of patience and energy. You have to learn what is good, what is brilliant, what has magic and what is merely workmanlike.

I am, in short, asking you to make brilliance a benchmark. In any interview for a marketing job you are almost certainly going to be asked to give examples of brilliance that you or others have created. You'll be asked about brilliant PR, advertising, digital. Your excitement and enthusiasm will get you the job because people want brilliant people working for them, especially in tough times.

CHAPTER 2

Have you got
the right stuff
to be a
marketer?

First things first

You need to take a long, self-critical look at yourself in the mirror

Marketing is as much about you and your personal strengths as it is about the marketing weapons available to you. Maybe you don't have all that it takes right now but if you know what it does take, you can work on it and turn yourself into a brilliant marketer. Most of all be an optimist because the first golden rule of marketing is that nothing is impossible.

> the first golden rule of marketing is that nothing is impossible

Unfortunately, because everyone's trying so hard not to fail nowadays, very few people are doing anything brilliant. Marketers are behaving more like engineers rather than the magicians they need to be. To be brilliant we need those people doing our marketing and orchestrating marketing campaigns to be inspirational, not merely adequate.

The core strengths that you need to have

So here are the some of the characteristics of brilliance – do you have them? More importantly what does it take for you to get them?

Do you open your eyes, ears and mind?

Do you spend at least five days a month out of your office – visiting shops or talking to customers and consumers? Do you meet lots of people who have stuff to teach you … are you shameless about gathering ideas from other people? Do you talk to people in the press who are often surprisingly knowledgeable? Do you meet your competitors? Do you enjoy what is often called 'the front line'?

Do you think new is cool?

Are you a fan and champion of anything and everything that is new and interesting? It doesn't have to be in your own market but it needs to have that 'edge' which makes you feel intrigued. Maybe it could have a spin-off in what you are trying to do. Remember that no one who is a dyed-in-the-wool, conservative thinker is likely to be brilliant at marketing. So sharpen your appetite for the unexpected or novel.

Do you really want to raise that bar?

Do you constantly ask yourself, your suppliers and your colleagues how you could do the marketing for your brands, products or services much better, so as to give it an electric impact in spreading the word about your brand? Are you ambitious? Are you demanding of others? Be demanding but don't be unfair. Those around you can only achieve the heights I am describing if you give them a climate of unconditional trust and the motivation a brilliant parent gives a five-year-old. Do not believe the 'no pain/no gain' myth which is propagated by marketing masochists. One of the greatest beer campaigns ever (for Heineken) was first conceived by a creative man lying on a sun-drenched, sandy beach. Sandy beaches and great long lunches are brilliant; misery and sandwiches in front of a PC are not so good. Wanting to improve is addictive. You'll find you love it.

> be demanding but don't be unfair

In summary, do you dream, do you want to dream and can you dream?

Can you visualise what your successful marketing campaign looks like; I don't mean literally, but how do you see it coming out – big and dramatic or slower burn – a building campaign or an explosive one? And do you like roller coasters? Because there's one thing your campaign must have and that's massive momentum. Changing things is never easy, but change is what marketing is all about. And change, like winning, is great fun. So get dreaming about a great sales-transformative campaign.

All good marketers have right and left brains in balance

Marketing is an art but with a bit of science thrown in. If you are going to be as good as you can, you need to have great intuition and the ability to forensically dissect an issue. You need to be a huge optimist and a realist. You need to know when to gamble and when to cut your losses. You need to be adept at separating the wheat from the chaff, yet at the same time be good at using and interpreting research. This may seem a bit of a juggling act, but all the best marketers seem to have this facility to shift focus from artist to scientist. Here are the things to work on to achieve mastery of the marketing mindset.

Do you really like people?

I mean *really* like them. Are you gregarious? Are you a people watcher? Are you a student of human nature? Do you find the way people decide to do something and then change their minds fascinating rather than frustrating? Understanding what makes people tick is the key to being a good marketer.

Do you have strong parental instincts?

Every project you are given, every client you have, everything you look after in marketing is your baby. There really is something essentially paternal or maternal about a marketing project;

and it's quite right that this should be so. After all isn't this *your* 'baby' whom *you* want to launch triumphantly into the world?

Do you like your colleagues?

If you don't like them, move on. Marketing is not a solitary pursuit: it's a team game. The smartest and nicest and most loyal people with whom I have worked were my colleagues. They made me perform better than normally. I made them perform. Together we were brilliant. I loved my colleagues. I really did. Working with them was exciting.

Could you do without your PC?

In a people-business brilliance can't exist behind a PC alone. We all of us spend an increasing amount of time behind our PCs dealing with hundreds of emails, working on spreadsheets, processing stuff. It's time to start looking people in the eye; time to inspire and be inspired; time to listen and time to talk; time to have ideas and time to be brilliant or try to be brilliant.

Why, why, why, why? Are you a question machine?

Are you a questioner never taking anything for granted or at face value? If so keep on asking questions. If you don't understand something or why a particular thing has happened, say so, especially if the news seems surprisingly good. This is the time to be deeply suspicious. Develop a huge curiosity. You'll have a much nicer time and be better at your job.

Do you really love detail?

After talking about big picture stuff and being above the battle, it's the detail that makes the difference. You need to be a great juggler and if you don't think you're that good at detail to start with, get good at it. Then, when you've proved you are good at it, surround yourself with people who are supreme at it. The best at detail I've ever seen, like Tony O'Reilly or Rupert Murdoch, are train-spotters when it comes to detail. Great architecture is built on carefully positioned stones.

Are you good in meetings where ideas fizz and challenges are tough?

Marketing people like to take control at meetings and they often love the interplay of ideas and they even like the friction. Meetings are great fun because they put people on their mettle. Meetings at their best are great because they are idea generative. Meetings above all need to end with a burst of positivity which marketers are good at. Remember 'nothing is impossible'.

Are you bursting with energy?

I never yet met anyone any good at marketing who wasn't fizzing with ideas and bursting with get-up-and-go. You are going to be a tiring person and a tired person. But you are also going to get a lot out of life, your job and the people you work with if you have that buzz.

Do you really instinctively know what brilliant is?

John Neill, CEO of Unipart, said, 'People in the UK don't know what good is.' They didn't in the 1970s and 1980s, but they do know now. And they really are beginning to know what brilliant is. And the good news is we've always been smart at marketing. The challenge now is to prove we can excel at it – not just be good at it but get to that next point, that A* level.

Do you like shopping?

Enjoy seeing the very lifeblood transaction of your career being transacted in shops. There's a magic moment when you see your brand being bought. It's the rustle and chink of money that any brilliant marketer finds the sexiest sound.

I hate the word competent and so should you

Our world today is competent.
It is also interesting.
It is efficient.

It is fit for purpose.
It is satisfactory.

(And aren't all these dull old words? Nothing to fire us up here.)

It's because everyone's trying so hard not to fail that there are very few people doing anything brilliant. Everything is a bit second-class. Marketers are behaving more like the engineers rather than the magicians they need to be. To be brilliant we need those people doing our marketing and orchestrating marketing campaigns to be inspirational, not adequate. People who can engage with others.

Well, don't you believe the consumer needs and deserves to be inspired? You're a consumer yourself – how do you feel?

 **brilliant** tip

Imagine selling your brand or an unfamiliar product to someone you've never met before. Think about how you'd inspire them.

How to sell something and feel that buzz

You'd be enthusiastic and friendly; you'd talk in user-friendly, non-technical language in order to reach people at their level; you'd show how the product solved the problem you imagined they had. Most of all you'd have to get and then keep their attention. A bit of drama and product demonstration wouldn't go amiss. Above all, you'd want to show you really loved that product and really wanted them to love it too.

This exercise is about being hands-on and getting out and about, seeing, hearing, smelling and touching the world around us. Marketers need to be salesmen, analysts, book-keepers and creative story-tellers all in one.

They also need to be distinctive.

When others zig, zag

You need to be unpredictable. In a competitive world, making it easy for others to anticipate what you are likely to do next really isn't smart. So here are some pointers on how to zig and zag.

Take a piece of paper. Draw a line down the centre; in the left-hand column write 'us' and in the right-hand column write 'competition'. Write down your five-point plan and then what you would do if you were the competition.

Now rewrite your plan making 'right-hand column's' job much harder.

Now write down an action on your part that might really wrong-foot your competitor. For example, increasing your quality and reducing your price, or increasing or reducing your marketing except in – say – trade promotions. The art of being counter-intuitive can provide dividends. Learn it and be a tricky competitor.

So far so good. But this isn't just a question of whether you have the raw material which can be carved and shaped to make you a brilliant marketer. You can and must learn from good people around you. Especially from some of the senior figures in the business who've seen it all.

Learning from the stars

One of those marketers with special talent is John Hegarty (actually Sir John Hegarty), founder of the very successful British advertising agency, Bartle Bogle Hegarty. He is worth quoting for his sheer common sense and refreshing, ordinary down-to-earthness:

You must understand that I am cursed with being an incorrigible optimist . . . I work because I love it. I'm genuinely interested in stuff. I love staying alert and keeping an open mind. The thing that ages you more than anything else is closing down, having a fixed point of view . . . [advertising has] entered the world of fashion where creativity and innovative thinking are paramount.

Peter Brown, who runs the toy company Flair, and used to run Tomy (UK), simply knows more about his market than anyone else – a classic case of knowledge is power.

Enter Rachel Bell, CEO of Shine Communications. Young, a mother of three, a powerhouse who is totally compelling, convincing and committed. With her, PR suddenly moves centre stage. No wonder Shine wins so many awards. Her big lesson is to love her clients, be in business partnership with them and be tireless in trying to improve.

Tony Simmonds-Gooding used to run Whitbread. Under his management the famous 'Heineken refreshes the parts', Stella Artois 'Reassuringly expensive' and R.White's 'The secret lemonade drinker' campaigns were born. The lesson he taught every marketer was to create the environment where great work is expected and encouraged and the result was very often great work was created. The very best in his case.

One of the most inspiring young men I've worked with is Ian George, MD of Twentieth Century Fox. Ian is the most wonderful story-teller. Nothing he describes is ever ordinary. He is also a truly great marketer who has two great expressions. 'I can't bear leaving money on the table.' Meaning – hating not to maximise the potential in a product or a film (in his case). 'You've got to keep trying to get better right up to the wire just in case a better idea comes along.' Tell stories well, set targets and hit them and never stop trying to do better. That's really great advice for all of us.

Finally, Napoleon who exclaimed when his adjutant gave him the rundown on the skills, experience and ability of candidates for a vacant post, 'Bring me lucky generals.' You can't find a formula for luck, but we've all worked with people who had the Midas or the anti-Midas touch.

All the above, Napoleon apart, are Midas people.

Getting by, getting on and going places

This tries to get under the skin of what makes the difference between chalk and cheese, between ordinary and brilliant, between Justin and Bob. Put yourself in a situation like theirs.

Justin was blessed by having the one advantage most of us would have prayed for in the womb had we been smart enough: Wealthy parents.

He led an indulged and comfortable childhood before being despatched to boarding school and then Tonbridge where he excelled at everything, scoring more runs than the youngest Cowdrey, more tries than Ben Ransom, more A*s than anyone in the history of GCSE, more As at A level than Einstein would have got, more curtain calls for his Hamlet than Branagh, more girlfriends than Casanova. He then got a place at Christchurch to read History and eventually, an inevitable, congratulated first.

In short Justin was insufferable and headed for the stars. So it was a surprise to everyone when he went on the graduate training course at Publicis, the advertising group, and set off on a career in marketing. But at least by joining a French group he could get to use his utterly flawless French.

He was doing really well, having the unusual ability to intimidate clients and bosses alike until he got a rather abrupt shock in one of his appraisals which said,

'He's brilliant as an operator but utterly devoid of any curiosity as to what makes people tick. This means he's a really hopeless marketer; completely clueless. Should be in investment banking where he can get rich using his own brand of accomplished bullshit.'

And that's where he ended up – in a big job at Lehman Brothers in 2008.

And now for Bob. Not born so much with a silver spoon as a tin spoon in his mouth.

Bob came from a family that never quite made it to middle class. Just as they were about to make that leap, that 'Ford Cortina breakthrough', his father got made redundant. At school Bob was a rather average, but a popular student. He was very often tired by working in the local Indian grocery store which he did most evenings, but he was seldom tired through intensive study. 'I'm an agnostic when it comes to work,' he said. His mother was a primary school teacher who got him to help her with her wall charts and cutting up magazines for her mobile boards.

His school report was cryptic 'he amuses all around him, however, his efforts in preparing for his exams are no cause for mirth'. When he got a stream of As and Bs at GCSE everyone apart from him seemed astonished.

'Don't be stupid – you aren't bright enough to go to Oxbridge,' the headmaster said when Bob applied, and was totally perplexed when the wretched boy got a place at Gonville and Caius to read English – 'He'll never get the three As,' he muttered darkly. 'Being able to wangle yourself through an interview is one thing, but exams will show him up ... '

But he did get his As and he did get in. And then he went mad. He performed in the *Footlights*, wrote a very bad novel, became President of the JCR and had huge fun, although he did only get a third.

In the long vacations he worked for Tesco and did rather well there.

When he came down he joined Publicis as a graduate trainee, did brilliantly and got swiftly promoted and it was he who appraised poor Justin. 'That guy was such a banker,' he reflected when he'd gone. 'He hated people and loved money. No soul; no insight.'

Bob is now next in line to Maurice Levy and still doesn't speak a word of French, but they speak of his marketing nous with awe ('*formidable et incroyable*').

The reason marketing is simply so much fun is that in marketing you have it in your power to transform a business. No other internal or external function can do that in the same way. That is what makes you feel powerful and why you actually are powerful. So standing in front of that mirror, decide whether you want to be Justin or Bob. You have it in you to be a Bob if you work really hard at the mindset characteristics described in this chapter. Go shopping, be good company, ask lots of questions. But most of all recognise that this is a big, big job you've got.

> in marketing you have it in your power to transform a business

CHAPTER 3

The marketing battleground – past, present and future

The past

Henry Ford said nearly 100 years ago:

History is more or less bunk. It's tradition. We don't want tradition. We want to live in the present, and the only history that is worth a tinker's damn is the history that we make today.

(Chicago Tribune, 1916)

Wrong, Henry, because history can and does teach us a lot, and helps us avoid making mistakes. But here's the real clincher.

Amazingly, of the top twelve global brands only two, Microsoft and Google, were created after 1940 (McDonald's started in 1940). Even Nokia goes back to 1865.

Which means you can't understand marketing without having a flavour of the past.

So how has marketing changed recently, over just the past 60 years?

The six ages of marketing

1950s – The dawn of modern marketing

Remember that food rationing after the Second World War only ended in 1954. But thereafter a lot happened. The first TV commercial was shown in the UK in 1955 for Gibbs SR toothpaste.

'It's tingling fresh. It's fresh as ice. It's Gibbs SR toothpaste.'
This is when the retail revolution, with the emergence of supermarkets and a consumerist economy, started leading to Prime
Minister Harold MacMillan's phrase 'we've never had it so
good'. Marketing and advertising had become almost
respectable as a sector in which to work (but not quite yet).

1960s – Mass marketing develops

This was the 'swinging sixties'. Carnaby Street, The Beatles and
The Rolling Stones, the sunshine flooding on to Manchester,
Birmingham, Liverpool and Newcastle – the home of The
Animals and 'The House of the Rising Sun'. TV advertising
became much more important. This was the era of promotions
like that with free plastic daffodils being given away as an incen-
tive. A time when soap powders went into combat rather like
jousting knights – *'have at thee with my free offer, a touch, a palpable
touch with my advertising jingle'*. Breakfast cereals contained
plastic toys. In supermarkets there were people dressed up as
Honey Monsters sampling Sugar Puffs. Amazing prizes like
tartan Mini Minors sat surrounded by tonnes of Scott's Porage
Oats. Atora Suet was a big brand in this suet-soaked age. Bisto
was a power KPI – key price indicator. Fine Fare was a very big
supermarket. Even the Kray twins had a small (but unsurprisingly
aggressive) promotional company. Everyone was at it. Marketing
was cool. Marketing was swinging. Marketing was mainstream.

1970s – Creative marketing arrives

Advertising was the marketing driver in the 1970s and a series of
impressive advertising agencies hit the UK – Saatchi & Saatchi,
BMP, French Gold Abbott, WCRS, one of the founders of
which, Robin Wight, pronounced his intention 'to kick away the
white sticks of the big, fat US agencies'.

Advertising became increasingly sophisticated, with campaigns
for Heineken ('It refreshes the parts that other beers can't
reach') and Hamlet cigars ('Happiness is a cigar called Hamlet')

both from the best agency ever but now disappeared – CDP. Advertising that had delivered the three 'b's – 'big, bland and boring' – was scorned by the bright young stars like Ridley Scott, David Putnam, Alan Parker and Adrian Lyne, all of whom started their lives in advertising.

1980s – The decade of the 'brand'

Big became beautiful. Marketing became a golden key to unlock fortunes. Research companies had never been so rich. New products were filling the shelves. The UK took over the world with WPP buying US bastions like J Walter Thompson and the Ogilvy group. Marketing became a zero sum game with warfare breaking out in product sectors everywhere. There was even a 'lawnmower war' every spring between Flymo and Ransome who declared their rotary product was 'much less bovver than a hover'. The brand became the thing. In 1988 RHM were under threat of a hostile take-over and they hired Interbrand to help recast their balance sheet by revaluing their brands. The three 'b's had become big, branded and belligerent.

1990s – Target marketing

The way it used to work was the advertising agency retained a commission of 17.65 per cent on all media bought. And the way media people were treated in agencies was as though they were 'below stairs'. They were always last on in new business presentations. They were regarded as a necessary evil but rather good at maths. And maths was now what was needed. The world had become a complex place with an explosion in media choice and consumers breaking into niches. It was no longer a case of 'whack it on telly'. Clients were becoming cleverer, many with MBAs, and were asking awkward questions about models for effectively deploying funds and things like ROI. When the word 'creativity' was mentioned, they'd ask, 'What are the measurement matrices?' and puce-faced creatives would make for the pub. So media men took over. The commission system collapsed

:ms always do (good to bear that in mind). And the
all about precision targeting and value for money.

2000s – Digital marketing

Enter a new pretender. The digital-space-kid whom Richard
Eyres (ex Capital Radio, ITV, Pearson and the Guardian Group)
once described as being very spotty, with lots of body piercing
and a permanent expression of rage on his face. His mission was
not to be leading edge or cutting edge but 'bleeding edge'.
Suddenly if you weren't spending half your budget on the web
you were a dinosaur. Search Engine Marketing was where the
cash was going. It was the equivalent of derivatives and hedge
funds to most marketers – they didn't understand a word but it
sounded good. Everything had a number against it and there was
a refreshing DIY element attached. The priests of marketing had
had their liturgy removed; but there was something missing.

It was the 'idea'.

What's next? That 'big' idea.

Next – the age of the 'idea'. What an exciting time to take up or
be involved in marketing when what everyone wants is an all-
embracing idea that can be translated into whatever medium or
type of marketing that you choose. That 'big' idea that will be the
most powerful concept for 50 years.

Everyone is looking for the idea that is probably global and that
certainly integrates all activities. It'll be an idea you can easily
summarise – like Pimm's and sunshine, like Bisto and roast
lunch, like Google and search, like Amazon and the world's best-
stocked bookshop, like Aga and the heart of the home or Ben &
Jerry's and yum, yum.

Meanwhile, let's not forget that this is a contest which used to be
well mannered, but has now become increasingly adversarial.

The present: some facts of life

Fact: Fewer people watch any one TV channel. (In 1965 in the US just three prime time TV spots were needed to reach 80 per cent of the population. Today it is around 100.)

Fact: TV is very expensive now. (Is it affordable with TV advertising costs having gone up 250 per cent in the past decade?)

Fact: Returns from advertising are poor. (It's estimated that less than 20 per cent of TV advertising generates of positive ROI.)

Fact: People skip ads. (90 per cent of people who can skip TV ads do so.)

Fact: There's a lot of advertising. (Daily exposure to advertising messages exceeds 3000 a day.)

Fact: Nobody's got enough time. (So many magazines, web pages, radio and TV channels, posters and chuggers and people dressed up as teddy bears.)

While I have always distrusted the dogma of a volley of factual bullet points like this (as you should), we all know that these are all pretty well spot on. Mass marketing used to be affordable when £1million bought you a decent, national TV campaign with a little poster money left over. But that era is long, long past.

Consumers are hard to reach. They are expensive to reach, and just when you think you've reached them they turn you off. Hard to see how you can afford or justify a big marketing budget, but wait a moment.

Marketing factors of today and of yesterday

Here are four factors which shape the way we do things now. And they are mostly good news, just as transparency is good news in financial services. The bottom line is that quality will shine out; as it always should have done. Compare how things are now with a far less rich past.

Product quality

Yesterday's consumers were less demanding. We were so surprised to get a good product in the distant past that we – as consumers – really didn't ask that much. The Austin Allegro and Triumph Dolomite seemed good enough cars back then. Standards were lower. And what price health and safety? People smoked in restaurants and theatres, small boys put coins on railway lines and cake baking was a big activity.

Today product and design reigns supreme. There really are better mousetraps being built – as Ralph Waldo Emerson said in 1889: 'If a man write a better book, preach a better sermon or make a better mouse-trap than his neighbour, tho' he build his house in the woods, the world will make a beaten path to his door.' Look at Amazon's Kindle, look at iPhone, look at Dyson, look at BlackBerry and look at Heinz Tomato Ketchup. All great and distinctive products. Brilliant marketing today involves spending as much time worrying about the product, how it looks, feels, tastes, smells and performs as it will on considering where its existence is broadcast.

Language and relationships that are authentic

Yesterday there was subservience to the establishment. Anchormen on radio and TV were craven in dealing with their leaders: 'Prime minister, sir, did you have a good holiday?' Now the reverence with which we treated ministers and monarchy in the past seems so strange. It was David Frost who ended all this.

Today marketers have got to speak 'people' not 'corporate'. Like it or not (and most senior corporate executives I talk to don't seem to like it at all) consumers are now in charge. They're in charge because they own today's primary medium, the web. Companies can't control what's on there. If you search for any company with the words 'bad news' attached you'll find yourself getting into a morass of grumbles. BMW may say it's a great car but ten angry customers of theirs can obliterate the value of their shiny advertising in minutes.

We don't live in a world of shiny-car-marketing any more – we live in a world of stock-car-marketing.

I loved a book called *The Cluetrain Manifesto* (2000) written by Rick Levine, Christopher Locke, Doc Searls and David Weinberger. In it the four authors say 'talk is cheap' (which it is today); talk is what modern technology has turned into a commodity. And this from Rick Levine, ex-Sun Microsystems:

People talk to each other. In open, straightforward conversations. Inside and outside organisations. The inside and outside conversations are connecting. We have no choice but to participate in them.

For years brochure writers have been trying, in a pompous, patronising kind of way, to speak to their audience rather as if they were Coriolanus in the Globe Theatre. But consumers now want to be spoken to in the language of today's consumer not the language of yesterday's proprietor. There is one stage beyond the 'Knowledge Economy' that we have just entered and it's the 'The Real Presentation Age'. Sure the product has to be great; but a *real* human being – one of us – has to present it engagingly and sell it with conversational passion.

Mass marketing was noisy: is dead

Yesterday we interrupted people with our story. We took up a megaphone and blasted our marketing message to whoever was out there to hear it. We used grapeshot. It is what we call 'interruption marketing' and it worked because TV was cheap and consumers put up with being interrupted.

Today we have more knowledgeable conversations. Don't you, for instance, imagine that Nike could have got the sports thing as right as they did if they hadn't spent a huge amount of time with athletes – soaking up locker room gossip. Don't imagine the John Lewis Partnership could be as successful as it is without brilliant people management, which involves a high level of interest in everyone who works there. An internal love affair leads to an external communication of it.

From management to leadership to heroes

Yesterday we were in manufacture. We didn't have CEOs, we had Managing Directors. Leadership was something we expected from admirals and generals, not businessmen. Sales was more important than marketing and required the gift of the gab not leadership.

Inspiring leadership is on everyone's agenda now. Steve Jobs, Phil Knight, Eric Schmidt, Larry Page and Sergey Brin are the heroes of the twenty-first century ... true role models. All recognise the role of innovation and creativity. The marketing and creative community consists of creative prima donnas. To get the best out of them calls for a level of leadership seen in orchestras and demonstrated by the Simon Rattles of this world. You need wizards but you also need impresarios. Great impresarios are usually great leaders.

 brilliant tip

Marketing today is about being heard above the white noise that prevails. This does not mean you have to be louder. But it does mean you have to be transmitting at the right frequency for your audience to hear you.

Current marketing is about change

If you can't change and enjoy it you'll find marketing hard, but you *can* change if you focus on the need. It just means there are a lot of things to do at the same time.

We are all required to do more and more stuff including multi-tasking. But in case you feel unduly guilty about not being very good at this, here's what David Weinberger said (again in *The Cluetrain Manifesto*). It's a prescription for a better life: focus is in; multi-tasking is out:

'The sum total of attention is actually decreased as we multitask. Slicing your attention, in other words, is less like slicing potatoes than slicing plums: you always lose some of the juice.'

brilliant tip

Save the juice.

Not enough money? You can still win

In a world where the marketing funds are never enough and often seem to be running out, there are still pockets of invest-ment that produce a powerful cut-through; and situations where real change is achieved through real cleverness. Like taking a brand – Lucozade – which was firmly positioned in the sick room, probably next to the chamber pot, and repositioning it as an energy drink. Exit invalid, enter Daley Thompson. Volumes soared. A niche, slightly negative, medical brand, something you 'took' rather than drank, became a positive healthy drink.

No one is impervious to change today. Not even the mighty Sony, under threat from the left by Apple's iPod and from the right by Amazon's Kindle. And this is exciting – not especially

have a better product and you too could be a winner

for Sony but for the new world order of brands. Back to Emerson; have a better mousetrap, have a better product and you too could be a winner. Just being big and rich no longer guarantees success.

However, the core lessons of history are these:

- boring communication seldom works;
- your reputation helps but alone is not enough;
- every marketing plan needs an idea not just money;
- we can learn from some of the enthusiasm of the past however naive it may seem today;
- we have to learn how to talk to our consumers on their terms not ours.

Orvis again, but I repeat this so many times because it is the key marketing mantra: 'Your customer's right even when he's wrong.'

The future

It was Sam Goldwyn, the film magnate, who reflected it was very hard to predict – especially when it comes to the future. What follows is therefore not so much an exercise in crystal ball gazing as a practical reflection on likely change and how the marketer of tomorrow will have to deal with it then and prepare for it now.

External factors

There's not a lot we can do it about these but there's no point in sticking our head in the sand. We shall see increasing unpredictability in this increasingly global world. Moscow, Shanghai, Beijing, Mumbai, Delhi will be (already are) just as important as

New York, London, Paris, Bonn. We shall see swings, booms and busts like never before. Nothing is impossible.

We live in a 24-hour society. Offices like Google's in Zurich are open 24/7. There will no longer be time to reflect for a few weeks. Response times will need to get faster so we'd better get used to it.

The corollary to unpredictability and change is the likely emergence of many more new opportunities previously not considered possible.

To realise them we shall not need to be super-strategists but master tacticians who are comfortable in constantly changing course.

The brilliant marketer is going to need to be athletic and agile.

Marketing methodologies

In looking at history, we have actually seen relatively little change apart from the rise of digital in the past 60 years; very much a case of evolution, not revolution. That is likely to change with media competition hotting-up with more customised papers and magazines produced at electrically topical speed and even some upbeat 'good-news' sheets to counter the ministry of doom that typifies Wapping today.

New technology will make experiential marketing much more of an experience; there'll be much more interactive marketing, virtual reality will become a reality and transform e-commerce, there will be more extraordinary cinematic experiences than ever conceived, making this and theatre too the new must-see.

The O2 and Wembley are just the beginning when it comes to live entertainment.

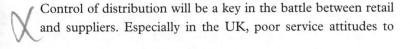
Control of distribution will be a key in the battle between retail and suppliers. Especially in the UK, poor service attitudes to

consumers will get punished. Ethical retail will flower – the Co-operative movement and John Lewis – as will e-commerce.

The key lever will be the building of relationships between consumer and brand owner. The concept of the lifelong customer more talked about than enacted at present will become central to all marketing. We may even see something long overdue –

> the concept of the lifelong customer will become central to all marketing

what I call rather flippantly 'relation-shops' – where customers are treated as friends and recognised by new identification technology, where shopping becomes a personal service experience.

A few changes. What can you do about them? Study anything that is new. New retail; new web technology; new debates about the politics of relationships – wholesaler, retailer, supplier, consumer; new discoveries and inventions – how many have you seen this year? Read all the trade papers, *Marketing Week*, *Marketing, Campaign, PR News*; look at Trendwatching and Springwise – the leading innovation spotters – you'll find them through Google.

Tune in to change and store anything interesting away. It'll come in useful.

Corporate challenges and issue

The face of business will change. In a global economy there will be an increasing emphasis on quality and value for money, which is going to hit high-inflation China hard. When Steiff, the soft toy manufacturer, took production back to Germany from China, saying an eye half a millimetre out turned Teddy's look of devotion into one of idiocy, it was a statement about China's inability to match German quality standards.

Corporate social responsibility is going to become more important. Diageo run marketing campaigns on the need for responsible drinking, not cynically, but because not to do so is to put their relationship with government and society at risk and because, anyway, it needs doing.

Brand partnerships will grow. Expect more and more alliances like Weight Watchers from Heinz. Imagine some others: Nestlé and Fitness First; Bose and Fox; Apple and Orange (I like that one); WHSmith and local schools and so on.

SMEs (small and medium sized enterprises) are going to grow rapidly – governments regard small and medium sized businesses as the true engine of the economy. With them there'll be a mass of new brands, and with those will come an increasing need for sharp marketing.

Which brings me to an interesting speculation about talent.

Talent in marketing rather than talent in finance is going to be seen as key in the next decade.

The brilliant marketer of the future who is very creative, fast on their feet and makes things happen is going to be highly prized and highly rewarded.

The change in consumers

Understanding what is changing and the obvious gaps in expertise seems a useful point of focus. Like the increasing importance of women as the decision-makers in the home and the key influencers over all purchasing decisions. But you wouldn't think that when you see an average car dealer at work would you?

Like the increasing importance of those over 55 as purchasers – you know the ones who feel about 40 and act about 30 – this is what American trend-watcher Faith Popcorn calls 'down-ageing'. When everyone in marketing is getting younger this potentially creates a problem of communication. And a marketing opportunity. And here's how. Go and talk to a group of older citizens and listen to what they say and what they want. Everything from bigger print to brighter light to less packaging to better manners.

In a lecture he gave to the University of Laguna at Google, Zurich, in October 2008, Wally Olins wryly noted that the consumer is 'answering back'. Brands, services, retailers that don't deliver are going to have an increasingly tough time. The web is a very public place where a snowball of a mistake becomes an avalanche of rage. Just check out Tesco bad news, BMW bad news, GWR bad news, BBC bad news, BT bad news or anyone bad news on Google. It's a revelation. But what an opportunity! At South Western Airlines in the USA they have a permanent and senior member of staff who sorts out all complaints as and when they are made.

Marketers will have a tougher time with consumers but this means you have to build better relationships and have more civilised, straightforward and intelligent conversations. Spend an hour looking around and trying to identify bad examples of marketing and decide why they occurred and what you would have done had you been in charge.

The blue sky and beyond

Local communities are going to grow in importance and a reversal of the demolition of local shops and pubs and post offices is surely on the cards. Look at the boom in allotments. Most councils have long waiting lists. Ask if people want a better local infrastructure.

If they want it, it'll happen.

The small business and family business boom is going to continue.

Provenance is going to become much more important.

Where it was made and the name of the QC inspector will

matter. Waitrose and M&S tell you where a lot of their fresh produce comes from by name, by county, by town. Towns and counties are spending a lot of money on their own marketing just because of this.

Cultural festivals are booming – Brighton, Edinburgh, Cheltenham, Hay-on-Wye, Manchester – as is the desire to play an instrument, sing in a choir and be a literary critic, hence the boom in book clubs.

The future will be exciting, diverse and unexpected which is why the big corporations will have a tougher time.

Marketing is going to be at the very core of a future that is more responsive to what people want. The winners are going to be the smart, the attentive, the curious, the energetic, the determined and the optimistic.

there has probably never been a better time to be in marketing

So there has probably never been a better time to be in marketing.

CHAPTER 4

On brands and brilliance – how do they work?

This is a deliberately short chapter because the business of branding probably deserves a book to itself. So rather than fall between two stools I have taken the view that what you need is a quick overview of what a brand is and how it works.

The power of the brand

The really big brands like Coca-Cola, Kellogg's Corn Flakes, Heinz Tomato Ketchup, Andrex, Persil, Whiskas, Sony, Nike, Apple, Google have certain things in common. Ubiquity. Very high awareness. Strong qualities capable of inspiring confidence, approbation and even affection. Great brands don't let you down and are part of your life and are more than just functional products. Look at what happened when Coca-Cola dared to change their recipe. Proof that the brand belonged to the consumer not the manufacturer.

Tony O'Reilly defined a brand when he was CEO at Heinz as a product so desired that a customer would leave a supermarket if it wasn't in stock and go elsewhere for it.

But now it's getting a bit eccentric. Branding is applied to everything. And strange names seem to be a starting point. They've always been around. Screaming Yellow Zonkers – a yellow snack food in a black box. Crazy Oats – it was a breakfast cereal that changed colour when you added hot milk and tasted of raspberries. But now we have a Dutch advertising agency called

Strawberry Frog and a series of new brands – Sticky Ass Glue, Squidoo, Woomp. And anything can be a brand.

No, surely that can't be right.

I didn't know I was a brand!

Everything that moves nowadays is a brand. I'm a brand. You're a brand. Planet Earth is a brand. My cat's a brand. The bee is a brand. Linda Barker is a brand and describes herself in the third person. London Bridge is a . . . stop! My head hurts.

People who know nothing about marketing talk about brands, with the consequence that a lot of us could get very confused. So let's have simple definition time.

Definition time

A brand is a marketing artefact and is a product or a service with the following:

	YES IT HAS THIS
A unique name	
A logo	
A designed identity	
A reputation*	
A provenance	
Emotional meaning to the consumer*	
Something bought and sold	
Something created by man/woman	
Consistency	
Producer pride	
Availability	
Worth more than an unbranded product	

* if the brand is a new one does it have the potential to achieve this?

What a brand is

Branding is the process of creating a personality for a product or service using a consistency of design and self-description which gives the object a distinctive feel, look and competitive position.

> branding is the process of creating a personality for a product

People go to all this bother so that they can get paid more money for it than they otherwise would.

A brand is something the consumer feels emotionally involved with. A brand is something that is remembered by name.

brilliant tip

Study brands that you like so you can see how they created the idea and then developed it. (For instance Coca-Cola used the image of Santa Claus in a Coca-Cola red outfit in the 1930s, giving both the legend and the drink a huge boost. In other words Coke stole Christmas.)

Small brands can be sexy too

And smaller brands that have that crazy potential to grab the public imagination.

Brands like Ben & Jerry's, the launch of which gave such a shock to the smart marketers at Diageo that they sold off Häagen-Dazs before the erosion of sales that they expected set in. Sometimes a strategic retreat is the best answer to a compelling attack.

Brands like Innocent. A great brand run by great people with a great attitude – their HQ in a slightly grimy part of west London is called Fruit Towers.

Brands like Pimm's. It's the only drink that stands for something as positive as 'sunshine'. (Given which they have to explain why they launched Winter Pimm's. That's like Speedo marketing Arctic clothing.)

Brands like Peperami with that immortal line 'it's a bit of an animal'. Suddenly there was a new snack hero on the block idolised by the kids, and a Simpsons-type creation hit the airwaves and word of mouth took over.

Brands like Amazon who, after years of building an unprofitable database, now have a direct conduit from writer to reader that in a few more years or so will be impossible to break; and they have Kindle. Amazon has the buzz that success breathes – it knows about me – what I read, what I seem interested in, so yes, it cares, it really cares about me.

How to create a brand

For the purposes of the argument I am reflecting on a B2B start-up company but it could be for anything because the principles are the same. The components are these:

1 A name
Create a name. And yes it can be a bit silly but remember you have to live with it. Great names have the following components:

- **Authenticity** – Kettle Chips, Rachel's Organic Dairy, Fisher-Price, Brabantia, Penhaligon's.

- **Provenance** – Ben & Jerry's, Thursday Cottage, Sheepdrove Organic Farm, Loseley, Pilsner Urquell

- **Character** – LeapFrog, Mother, Jaguar, Sweaty Betty, Mandarina Duck, Big Bertha

You'll create your name by thinking and thinking and one morning you'll wake up and know it. Do not spend money on getting an expert to create the name unless you are a very rich company.

2 A logo

Nike for very little money got that 'swoosh'. What you need is maybe nothing or maybe a thing to aid memory – an illustration of the idea your company stands for.

- An artefact – Sir Bibendum the Michelin man, HMV, Johnny Walker

- Brilliant colours – Caran d'Ache, Google, Channel 4, Orange

- A symbol – the Hadfield's fox, the Bass Red Triangle and the line 'Reach For Greatness', the [yellow tail] wallaby

3 A design

Now it's time for an expert to come in. You are already on the road to creating an identity. You need someone to extend, develop and refine that identity. But make sure you brief them well.

4 An attitude

No one but you can create this. Decide exactly what it is that makes you better, inspiring and different. Keep trying to express it in fewer and fewer words. What is the essence you are trying to own?

5 Various faces

Express your brand on business cards, letterheads, envelopes, signs, posters, mugs, pencils and so on. As many places that, with wit, you can make it live. Developing your web site so it reflects your brand character is especially critical. There are a lot of good designers around.

6 Interaction

See if you can get your customers to respond and even to use your branded artefacts. If they like your branded mugs they may use them.

7 A developing personality

Every six months review where you are and see if you can develop your brand. Your office decorations; staff T-shirts; Christmas cards; golf balls, pads, pencils etc., etc. Development never stops. Have a regular 'brand and what we can do to make it sing more compellingly' meeting.

One brand that has been brilliantly developed over time is Nike. When it had a bad year Phil Knight, founder and CEO, was not reticent in blaming, apart from other things, boring advertising and marketing.

**brilliant** tip

Don't ever be boring. Learn from the maestro at Nike.

**brilliant** example

Here's a quick overview of the Nike story which describes brilliance in action. It borrows from a brilliant book by Robert Goldman and Stephen Papson called *Nike Culture: The Sign of the Swoosh* and from the experience of FCO and the people there who launched Nike in the UK, principally Richard French and Ian Potter.

Understanding your business is key

'We got the sweaty side of health and fitness with the romance of it as well.'

Phil Knight, CEO

In other words be authentic. And simple . . .

Q 'How do I improve my times?'

A 'Run faster.'

Brands depend on people

'There are three key themes to Nike's success. People, people, people.'

Phil Knight, 2004 Annual Report

And what they *believe* ... their values.

The Nike values

- Rebels and outlaws – always being the challenger (with morals) – spiky good guys
- Not afraid to fail – always trying
- Not too serious – winking at the customer
- A bit cocky – always walking with a bit of a swagger
- Diversity of voice – varying the pitch
- Anything is possible – there's no finishing line
- Action not words – and when words are used, only words which 'fire' action
- Sport is classless – anyone can be a winner
- Attitude beats strategy – diversions from strategy are OK
- Experience not textbook marketing – never ever that ... please.

How to get the values

Nike listens.

Nike spends time in the locker room, on the track, in the bar, talking, watching, changing their own minds as a result of what they hear ... (they are not behind their PCs).

Grassroots touch.

Having local sensitivity.

Not a boring seen-it-before communication campaign.

'Staying neutral in marketing is tough ... great brands let the market fill a blank sheet with meaning and folklore.'

(Wibberfurth, *Brand Hijack*)

A moving target.

Always innovating, changing, arguing.

Always listening for the maverick voice.

Always looking for what's next.

Nike knows where its customers are, what they think, how they feel and where they are likely to be next.

Brands depend on everything fitting together

'Brands like Nike tap into the basics and don't waste time on brand differentiation and stuff.'

(Wibberfurth, *Brand Hijack*)

'A new beauty has been added to the splendour of the world – the beauty of speed.'

Tammaro Marinetti, Italian playwright, Nike Annual Report 2004

Speed is beautiful in every business.

Great, challenging ads

With great strap lines

'Just do it'
'I can'
'Anyone, anywhere, anytime'

Here are some examples of their ads – sorry words only:

Nike speaks to specific targets – to the old and to women.

This is from Mia Hamm, US female soccer star.

'There's a time and a place for mercy.
And it isn't here.
And it isn't now.'

To the racially oppressed.

Nike's first ad for Tiger Woods.

'Hallo world.

I am the only man to win three consecutive US amateur titles.

There are still courses in the US where I am not allowed to play because of the colour of my skin.

Are you ready for me?'

Violence. Competition. Winning.

(One Nike ad said, *'Winning isn't the only thing … cha, cha, cha.'*)

Some more ads, all about the naked drive to succeed – each with a flick of cynical wit that gives them street cred.

'Also available to mortals.'

(Viv Richards holding a cricket shoe when he was by some way the best cricketer in the world.)

'There are two sides to a sprinter.

The side that wants to crush his opponents and leave them blue and lifeless by the side of the track …

… and the other, darker side.'

(Michael Johnson, 1996 Olympics)

'You can protect your eyes and your skull and your ribs and your knees and your liver and your spleen.

Or you can protect your lead.'

(Wilem Defoe, Champion Mountain Biker)

'If you're not there to win, you're a tourist.'

(Andre Agassi, Atlanta Olympics)

So when it comes to branding *just do it*.

Summary

The bean counters nowadays take a more reverential view of branding, understanding that brands are hugely valuable and that all the goodwill that marketing, PR, advertising and digital work creates doesn't just disappear once it's occurred, but it actually accrues to and builds the brand. In other words, all those years of Coke advertising add to the lustre of the brand like so many layers of polish. Beware the vandal with sandpaper or that piece of grit though. Brands are delicate and damage easily.

brands are delicate and damage easily

Some brands are special. They have been created. They are consistently reliable. They mean something to the consumer beyond being a product or service. For instance, BMW is more than a car while Vauxhall is pretty much just a car.

Smaller niche or challenger brands are increasingly beating bigger rivals through guerrilla tactics. They are often brave, cheeky and likeable to many through this characteristic. We like underdogs. We like people who try harder like Avis did – what a great line of theirs this was:

'When you are No. 2 you try harder. Or else.'

Brilliant brands create buzz and get talked about. Getting talked about and occupying brain space is not easy, but when you achieve it sales will follow, provided your product is good enough and priced right. The Nike trick is to use advertising as news. Something different happens in each ad, but one thing is consistent – the love and understanding of sport.

You cannot be brilliant at brand marketing without having an intimate knowledge of your product and all your competitors. It's not just that knowledge is power. It's that knowledge allows you to understand what your product category is really all about.

If you don't really understand exactly what makes your consumers tick you can't be brilliant. This is getting a bit repetitive. Sorry, but unless you know who is going to buy your product and why they are going to do so you can't create, let alone market, a brand.

You need to build a close coterie of brilliant people to feed your brain and imagination and inspire you. People who have years of experience working with brands. People who understand that brands have DNAs and that this is worth money.

Understand (and respect) the very essence and personality of what you've created. Be true to its values. Do not change it; reinforce its strengths and occasionally refresh it.

Enjoy the adventure and be brave. We do not live in easy times but there's one thing you can be sure of. If people don't notice you or talk about you, you are not going to do very well. But if you manage to distil your essential specialness and articulate it engagingly then you may be en route to creating a real, living brand. And brands really do live because they change and develop and grow. And, what's more, people enjoy them.

PART 2

Ladies and gentlemen choose your weapons

A journey around the different marketing techniques and how they can be made to work best and most economically.

We don't recommend DIY specialist marketing but here's how to cope with the 'experts' and how to DIY if you have no other choice.

CHAPTER 5

Advertising – the root of the great sales pitch

What advertising is

Advertising is about the art of dramatising a brand. Good advertising gives you reasons, rational and emotional, to consider or even buy a brand. Brilliant advertising seduces you and sweeps over you and sweeps you off your feet. The modern consumer is bored with most advertising, but the very best and most creative work is eagerly watched on YouTube. Advertising is still the most thrilling and moving part of marketing.

How advertising works

There is an important distinction to be made between ordinary advertising and the brilliant stuff that makes the hair on the back of your neck stand up. Ordinary advertising like musak or wallpaper passes us by and is easily avoided. The brands and their advertising that light us up, according to Martin Lindstrom (his book is called *Buyology*), literally light up our caudate nucleus in the same way that it lights up nuns' caudate nuclei when asked their fondest memories of God. Lindstrom literally and scientifically examines brainwaves, but to those of us who spent much of our lives in advertising, we too can define what makes the best advertising. And this is it:

- A good story well told
- An observation about us that is true

- A reminder of something familiar or loved
- Or as Alexander Pope put it 'what oft was thought but ne'er so well expressed'.

But does it really still work today?

Here's what Maurice Saatchi said in the *Financial Times* on 22 June 2006.

'Sometimes I feel as though I am standing at the graveside of a well-loved friend called advertising. The funeral rites have been observed. The gravediggers have done their work. The mourners are assembled. Most of them are embarrassed to say they ever knew the deceased. 'Advertising?' they say. 'I'm not in that business.' At the age of 50, advertising was cut down in its prime.'

Yes, advertising has been put under pressure by all sorts of alternative marketing, not least digital. Far fewer people watch TV so it's harder to reach mass audiences. But advertising still provides the motor power to a lot of marketing campaigns.

Advertising is the soul of marketing. It's the ignition to great ideas. Even if you don't spend a fortune on placing advertisements, going through the discipline of thinking about how to advertise will make you think harder and more effectively about how to sell your brand.

advertising is the soul of marketing

brilliant tip

You need to see of a lot of advertising and be a student of it. Advertising is an art and the best practitioners of it love advertisements. The more advertisements you see, the more you will understand how it works (and why, often, it doesn't work).

What has changed?

People consume advertising in a different way nowadays. Their attention span is much shorter. They are also advertising literate – which is to say they understand how it works and are peculiarly resistant to hard sell.

The current need, given this short attention span, is for a phrase or even a word which describes the emotional or functional property you are seeking to own. Advertising is not a world of long copy; it's a world of very fast ideas. Most of all, though, when it's done well, advertising is about ideas.

Unless we can define a piece of territory, a particular attribute or characteristic that we want to own and around which the advertising ideas and other expressions of marketing will spin, then we aren't working hard enough.

Wise and timeless words on what makes brilliant advertising

Possibly the greatest ad man of all time was Bill Bernbach, the founder of the agency Doyle Dane Bernbach. He was very opinionated.

Here's one of his opinions:

'However much we would like advertising to be a science – because life would be simpler that way – the fact is that it is not. It is a subtle, ever-changing art, defying formularisation, flowering on freshness and withering on imitation; where what was effective one day, for that very reason, will not be effective the next, because it has lost the maximum impact of originality.'

This idea of advertising being a cross between magic and art is appealing to anyone who has been there at the very coalface of creativity, seen an idea conceived and the impact it can have on consumer attitude and product sales. And the key is not just the 'what' of the idea, it is also the 'how' that idea is executed. And here's a brilliant tip from Bill:

At its core advertising is about great story-telling

Advertising is the source of most great marketing communication ideas, because over time the best story-tellers have very often been advertising men or women. Alan Parker, Ridley Scott, Adrian Lines, David Putnam, Fay Weldon, Salman Rushdie, Wendy Perriam, and so on, all started their careers in advertising.

The great, 'reassuringly expensive' Stella Artois campaign depended on simple but compelling and beautifully told stories always about the allure of the brand being too strong to resist.

Nestlé Gold Blend made an art of story-telling by taking a soap opera idea – 'Hallo neighbour, can I borrow some sugar?' into a complete new league – coffee as a passport to sex and possibly a longer-term relationship. So exciting that the PR value probably exceeded the advertising spend.

Mastercard is doing the same thing in brilliant press ads now with unwritten stories you have to decode. Mostly stories about successful parents dedicating love and time to buy things for their adored children – not so subtle green stain on sleeve and reference to Test Match ticket for son, Boyzone wrist bracelet for daughter's treat. All quite 'priceless', which it is when it works this well.

Great distillations of great brands

Advertising is great at making less achieve more. It is the art of précis and drama all in one. It has been brilliant at creating simplistic and memorable straplines and advertising lines like these which evoke affirmation and a smile:

- Paxo – Rooster Booster
- The *Independent* – It is. Are you?
- Wonderbra – Hello Boys
- Heineken – Refreshes the parts other beers cannot reach
- Honeywell – Designed well. Built well. Honeywell
- Swan Vesta – Britain's favourite old flame
- Levis – When the world zigs, zag
- Stella Artois – Reassuringly expensive
- Heinz – Beanz Meanz Heinz
- Toshiba – Hello Tosh, gotta Toshiba?
- BA – The world's favourite airline
- *The Economist* – How to win at board games
- Castrol – Liquid engineering
- *Ah Bisto!* – Those two urchins sniffing the air and getting the whiff of a delicious roast lunch is just so evocative. Like Guinness there's something iconic going on here with that wonderful toucan and the really terrible line *'if one is good for you just think what toucan do'* (it's they way they tell them!). Both Bisto and Guinness advertising had – and Guinness have since sustained the momentum with huge confidence and authority. A Guinness spokesman said recently that they spent a lot on their creative work despite the decline in audience levels on TV because if it was good enough it got seen and admired on YouTube. The references to Guinness advertising are certainly plentiful on this medium and well watched.

In the 1970s and 1980s advertising was elevated to a level of quite extraordinary importance. *'Labour isn't working'*, said Saatchi & Saatchi's poster for the Conservative Party, and this was claimed to have won an election no less.

The hip-swaggering peak of advertising

It was said, when advertising was at its peak, that consumers didn't drink the beer, they drank the advertising. And as brands like Foster's, Heineken and Carling Black Label populated the TV screens with better and better TV commercials one supposed this might be true.

brilliant tip

'If an idea makes me laugh that's a sure sign it's a good idea. All commercials should be entertaining, no exceptions made. Somebody's making the business too rational, which is wrong. Advertising is an emotional business ... everybody ought to have fun ... if you aren't having fun then you are getting screwed.'

(Lou Centlivre, Executive Managing Director, Foote Cone and Belding 1985)

The essential art

Advertising is a distilling process whereby we learn how to make a great sales pitch. Richard French, doyen of the trade, once said, 'I'm a professional liar: I used to work in advertising', but he was laughing as he said it. Advertising is a more theatrical form of salesmanship where all the senses are relentlessly seduced to get a result.

advertising is the engine of modern marketing

Bill Bernbach was right. Advertising is the engine of modern marketing and we should respect its subtlety and its power.

Despite a vast amount of work to prove how it works, it is an art not a science and even a pretty inexact art. When he spoke about mathematics, Bertrand Russell got it spot on. *'The subject in which we never know what we are talking about nor whether what we are saying is true.'*

But we can try.

Read and see

Look at the best ads on YouTube.

Watch www.adbrands.net

Read:

Campaign
D&AD annuals
The World's Best 100 Posters, Rob Morris and Richard Watson
Confessions of an Advertising Man, David Ogilvy
The Practice of Advertising, Normal Hart (editor)
Buyology, Martin Lindstrom

CHAPTER 6

How to make advertising work

Getting the message right

Putting all your eggs in one basket always seems risky, so if you do, watch that basket! I always advise people to use professionals to produce advertising – as with good design it is rare for an amateur to produce anything that has the power and freshness a professional will achieve. However, sometimes you have no choice. Here are a series of things to help if you are doing this yourself.

First of all read your brief. Five times. Your brief is your exam question. Take a big A2 pad and start to generate ideas. Short phrases; anything that catches the eye and is on the brief. After an hour or so hopefully you'll have a few thoughts that are worth pursuing.

brilliant tip

If you can, work with someone else sometime during this process to check what you are doing. This process is very much about two heads being better than one and a case of input helping to create output.

How people get their ideas

Like all artists they beg, borrow or steal them. As Picasso said, 'Amateurs borrow, professionals steal', but if you watch them, senior creative people in advertising agencies read more than most people, listen to more music, visit more art galleries, watch a lot more films than average. They are like blotting paper.

If you have an idea you like – it could be a headline or a picture – show it to your wife, husband, child, mother, father, friend, whoever and get a reaction. If in doubt, reject it. And reconcile yourself to a harsh reality of life. This is hard and may take quite a long time. But if you think you've cracked it, leave whatever you've done and come back to it 24 hours later.

brilliant tip

In the cold light of day what seemed genius at 11.30pm sometimes reveals itself in its true colours as being garbage at 11.30am the next day.

What hooks people?

It's about connecting with them; creating an echo in their brain; doing what nursery rhymes do to young children. It's about assonance or alliteration or rhymes or reference to something else or a piece of wit. The difference between two versions of one of the oldest advertising lines may seem subtle but it isn't:

You'll wonder where the yellow went
You wonder where the yellow's gone

The first one gets hooked into your mind that much faster because of the assonance of *yellow* and *went*. But the impact is all the greater and the whole line becomes unforgettable when you are told the brand is Pepsodent. This may not be poetry but it's great verse:

You'll wonder where the yellow went
when you brush your teeth with Pepsodent

A checklist

If you like checklists use the following:

- Is it on brief?
- Is it clear and understandable?
- Is it going to stand out?
- Is it expressed in a relaxed way?
- Is it memorable?
- What will it look like in context (for instance in a newspaper, on a wall, on someone's doormat)?
- Is it likely to sell anything?

If you're not getting ticks on this checklist then it's back to the drawing board. All of which is why, if you can afford it, using professionals is so much better. Their drawing boards are a better place than your drawing board, believe me.

> if you can afford it, using professionals is so much better

Making advertising agencies do great work for you

You don't get to work at an advertising agency unless you have what someone I know calls the 'smarts'. Jeremy Bullmore, who is one of the cleverest men to have been in advertising, describes creative people as wearing black T-shirts and looking permanently grumpy.

In my experience they are often quite insecure, wondering if they can still produce great work (or any work) and feeling only as good as their last advertisement. Although one told me his greatest terror was the next ad just wouldn't come. A bit like Sparky and his magic piano when the piano revolts and Sparky is exposed.

But account handlers, or 'suits' as some call them, tend to be smart and generally funny and self-confident, as most salesmen usually are. The people walking around looking very thoughtful and slightly pained are Planners and we'll deal with them on another occasion. They are too clever for the moment.

brilliant tip

Help those insecure creatives feel loved and rated. Ask that they have lunch on you, the client.

Agency relationships in general

Make sure of three things:

- That the agency values your business not just because you spend money with them but because you are appreciative of their skill and effort. Thank them a lot. Make them pleased that you are coming in to see them. Go out of your way to be popular and you can then be as demanding as you want, which should be very, very demanding.

- That they understand what you are trying to achieve in the long run not just on an ad by ad basis. Agency people are professionals and like dealing with people who have grand plans, who have a strategic vision. And they like feeling they are working in partnership.

- That they know you like good advertising and want to sponsor work that is cutting edge and not boring or ordinary.

Advertising checklist (don't leave home without it)

This is really important. More careers have been spoilt by being sloppy than should have been possible. This checklist stops you having an 'if only' moment.

1 The brief. Has it been agreed with all the key people in your organisation and at the agency? Make sure it is actually signed off, not just verbally agreed.

> more careers have been spoilt by being sloppy than should have been possible

2 Is what is produced good enough? Imagine you are a target consumer. Does it speak to you? Are you going to be proud of being the owner of this advertising?

3 Is what is produced on brief? Look at what is produced very carefully over a couple of days. If you have concerns, record them.

4 Do you have a proper internal approval system? If not, create one. Make sure all the people who need to see it do so.

5 Are there any corporate strategic issues? Is there anything someone senior might pick up on – some legacy in the place, however odd, like we don't have children or animals in our advertising? Or does the CEO have a prejudice about something – like Ernest Saunders did when he ran Guinness. He couldn't stand comedians. So he was told Billy Connolly was a social humorist not a comedian and this appeased him when he saw the Kaliber advertising.

6 Is it legal, decent and honest? Are there any conceivable IPA, ASA, Ofcom issues? Are we knocking competition unfairly? Could anyone in the media seek to ridicule us?

7 Are there any other issues? Is it going to create an issue with any of the trade customers or distributors? Is there any downside with the advertising from any quarter?

8 Have there been any advertising problems historically? What were they? What was the resolution?

9 Proofreading. Do it yourself. Check pagination. Leave nothing to chance. Dianne Thompson, CEO of Camelot, went to check proofs of a very important, long document at the printers – an arduous task and she found what would have been two embarrassing errors. That's leading from the front. And here's how to proofread properly:

- do it slowly
- read it backwards
- read it forwards
- then again.

10 Caveat. Do not expect anything from all your efforts if:

- the type is too small – people's eyesight deteriorates as they get older
- you have too much information and too many ideas in collision with each other.

Summary

- Don't do your own advertising if possible. It's nearly as bad as doing your own surgery. Messy, risky and possibly fatal. You should work with an advertising agency.

- Hopefully they'll be excellent. Only work with the very good practitioners of the art, sit with them, listen to them, learn from them and challenge them to be the best.

- Understand that this is a one-ball game. If I throw a consumer one ball they'll probably catch it, if I throw them two they'll probably miss both, and almost certainly all of them if I throw them three.

- Try to ensure that everyone doing work of any kind for you knows you are obsessive about having a unity of feel and look.

- Be dispassionate. Keep on asking hard questions. Especially, does this advertising sell my product?

- Be funny about fonts. Not enough time is spent by people seeing which fonts work and how. It's easy on a PC to simply take a piece of copy and see what happens to it in various different ways. Look at interesting, underused fonts like Garamond, Palatino and Comic and see what happens.
- See what happens
- See what happens
- **See what happens**
- Have that checklist and go through it absolutely rigorously.
- Condition those around you to expect challenging work that will sell a lot of stuff.

Conclusion

Be excited by what you are doing – this is great fun – and it's more fun because it isn't easy, so the satisfaction of doing it well is enormous. Remember the advertising idea and expression of the 'short-sell', that two-word equity – the piece of territory we are going to make unique for our brand – that distilled message for your product, service or brand which is the platform that underpins everything else. Get that right and you're nearly there on the road to brilliance.

CHAPTER 7

Where to advertise so it reaches the people you want to reach

All about media

use experts but have
very strong opinions

First of all, know your audience – describe them in detail. The choice of media today is such that you can be much more rifleshot than grapeshot in your aim. List your different types of audience: what they think, feel, do, aspire to, enjoy as hobbies. Really try to get inside their minds. We are way past defining people with boring old demographic titles (C2 female 35–45) – yes but what does she think and where does she live?

To be on line for creating the best media brief you can provide, you have to get a lot of information and have a lot of opinions about who precisely you are trying to reach.

Second, how much do you have to spend? How sensitive is this? Is that the maximum, minimum, anticipated, agreed or whatever budget? Don't do loads of work until this is clear.

Third, answer these questions:

- Your preferred length of campaign.

- Your preferences for media type and explain why (a professional will dissuade you if he genuinely thinks you are wrong).

- Explain your long-term strategy for your product and explain what this particular campaign is trying to achieve.

- How important is stand-out for you? Have you considered being very big, noisy and active with a smaller group rather than trying to reach a wider audience?

good media planning is not just about maths, it's also about imagination

- Have you thought about being counter-intuitive and trying to find a really unusual and creative way of achieving your goal? Good media planning is not just about maths, it's also about imagination.

- Be very sceptical about measurements like CPT (cost per thousand). Think more about cost per customer conversion – i.e. if you spend £x how many new users do you need and how much extra usage from existing users? Is this credible?

- The arithmetic on the relative impact of a double-page spread in colour and a half-page in colour suggest the former is twice as effective, but probably three to four times the cost. A study of rate cards gives you a working touch for relative costs – although no one buys at rate card because you can always negotiate a discount and play one medium against another. But beware being too cheeky if you are a very small advertiser. Business is business.

- The way in which you see the media schedule contributing to the momentum of the campaign – which components are designed to do what. Consider this is a building. What are the foundations? What is the roof?

Mainstream media

A quick gallop through the media scene with some opinion as to what is going on which may provoke some ideas.

- **TV** – the biggest sales tool ever invented. It's still the 'big boy' but use it with care and only if you have deep pockets. They actually used to have 'as advertised on television' by products in shops. It's now easy to be very precisely targeted because there are so many different channels. Advertising spend is declining and the major traditional channels were suffering in late 2008.

- **Cinema** – magnificent if you have the wit and creativity to compete with Hollywood films. You can't believe how young the audiences are, nor how involving and wonderful the scale of the experience is. Watch people as they come out – bright-eyed, red-cheeked and with flared nostrils. Cinema is a big experience.

- **Radio** – said by many housewives in research to be their best friend. An under-used medium. Surprisingly, not many creative people seem to enjoy writing radio commercials nor are they very skilled at it. But it's claimed around 75 per cent of people listen to radio at one time or another. This is the place for low cost campaigns that develop a strong story line over time with lots of different advertisements – think the radio equivalent of Gold Blend – a soap opera that captured the nation's imagination.

- **Posters** – patchy distribution makes it hard to reach many in places like Cambridge or Brighton but for me, done well, one of the classiest ways of making a statement. It's that view that makes it so important in political campaigns. Rule. If you are going to have more than a five-word headline there had better be a very good reason.

- **National newspapers** – this is where your ads become tomorrow's fish and chip paper. The best ads I've ever seen in newspapers were always newsy and topical like the ad for Champneys featuring a miserable-looking David Gower (England had just been thrashed by the West Indies) with the headline 'I wish I was at Champneys'. Context is all and I never saw any point in anything bigger than a page-dominant size. People buy papers to scan news not look at ads. Circulation is declining fast.

- **Magazines** – a totally different browsing world with a vast choice of specialist titles. Most are so dense with advertising you are really going to struggle unless your creative work is very strong. But the good news is there are lots of interesting ways of spending money and reaching pretty well exactly whom you want.

- **The web** – it has its own chapter, of course. Just make sure your web site works properly and through intelligent SEM make sure you are in the right place on the page – near the top.

Alternative media

- **Local newspapers** – the underestimated medium. The creative environment is often quite dull so standing out can be quite easy. But be local, using local outlets or people as heroes, if you are using the medium. Context is important – exploit it. But beware rapidly falling circulation.

- **Free sheets** – I am a deep sceptic but check out the prices and make your own judgement. There are some that are excellent and many that are not.

- **Local magazines** – focus on the feel and the quality of editorial; do not just rely on the numbers. I have always been choosy about the company with whom I'm seen. Don't get yourself tied up with a goodwill gesture when what you need is to save time and conserve cash.

- **Local radio** – I love it and think the real key here is not to be just an advertiser but – if you can afford it – to be a local 'player'. Look at it as a promotional medium and see how you can leverage your 'presence' as well as your campaign itself.

- **Posters** – repeated because it's like New York – a hell of a medium. You can achieve really strong local presence too. Advice: if you are focusing on a specific town make sure you know where the best sites are. The best sites are where people are waiting, at a station, in a predictable traffic jam, at traffic lights.

- **Transport** – if you can do something really interesting with buses or trains like RBS did with the Heathrow Express then that's terrific and expensive, and large sums can disappear to small advantage; but for little money in London, tube cards and cross-track can be absolute magic. It's one of the few chances to have people read your quite long copy because there isn't anything else to do while they are standing and wishing they were still in bed. Marketing to captive audiences is great fun too especially if you can make them laugh.

- **Events** – easy to get swept up in the excitement and find you are having a great time, but sales of your product remain disappointingly flat. Be ruthless. You are there to sell stuff so how can you turn an event to your advantage?

- **Theatre/event programmes** – generally advertising in these should go in the social corporate responsibility budget, if you have such a thing. A media man who was excellent at his job said they caused him so many problems in relation to the benefits they brought he made a rule to avoid them.

- **Videos/DVDs** – brilliant for mailing to 'warm contacts', these are the equivalent of film-letters and as such need to be punchy, brief and full of life. You need simplicity, good lighting, little distraction, your own people and a great piece of packaging.

Buying your media is risky

Same advice. If possible, find a professional to do it for you. But if you can't you are in the 'hot seat'.

Unless you are a great negotiator get someone else to do it for you. In life, avoid trying to be a 'one-man band'; the music you produce is usually terrible. But if there's no choice, get out your calculator, put on your ruthless shoes and start buying. Here are five pieces of advice:

1 **Be tough**. Develop a nasty sceptical laugh. No, I'm joking, just put on 'I'm a tough buyer' coat before you start.

2 **Be knowledgeable**. Only try and buy something when you have lots of information – the rate cards of your chosen medium and all the competitive media.

3 **Be smart**. Offer exclusivity for larger discounts and only if you think it's right for your product.

4 **Be professional**. Always keep the person you are buying from in touch with your decisions – this isn't personal, it's business. Always give them space to come back with a counter-offer.

5 **Keep it simple**. Don't ever try to orchestrate a programme of events which keeps you awake at night. What looks good on paper often looks horrible in practice because it's too complex to do properly.

brilliant tip

Spend a useful lunch with a media professional who will give you right up-to-the-mark opinions and facts about what is really going on in media.

Conclusion

This is all about money and measurement and getting enough bangs for your buck. This is about left brain and scepticism. A healthy cocktail in a heady world.

CHAPTER 8

PR – just give them the facts

How PR works

At its simplest, PR is about getting positive, fact-based stories about your company, its brand, its products and its people appearing in the media. But it's also about fending off and avoiding negative stories. It is now right at the centre of the marketing story because reputation has never been more important. As the founder of JP Morgan – JP Morgan himself – said,

'Our clients' belief in our integrity is our most precious possession.'

brilliant tip

Be obsessed with providing and proving you are providing great value for money. Always make the answer to the question 'so what did I get for my PR money?' a litany of good news.

What has changed

PR agencies used to be full of leggy lovelies drinking Bollinger and smoking Sobranie Black. All Absolutely Fabulous. But it was in the 1990s as business got more serious and the power of PR was appreciated more and more by the politicians that the PR world changed. It was the Alistair Campbells and Lord

Mandelsons of this world who realised the importance of the next day's news story.

PR is about solid, factual stories not puffery

You also need substance. Following the takeover of Safeway, Morrisons had about as nasty a time with the analysts and business media as could be imagined. Sir Ken Morrison was pilloried as a dinosaur and the whole management and data system of the group collapsed.

Enter Mark Bolland – urbane, Dutch, ex-Heineken executive – and within a year Morrisons was (in relative terms) the UK's best performing supermarket group with great results, a good story and something else that was magic called momentum. They even took on the OFT for untrue allegations about price fixing, won and were awarded damages.

PR became a professional business when people looked at clients with a view to enhancing their clients' businesses and not just having fun. No wonder *PR Week* has suddenly become such an important magazine. PR suddenly moves centre stage.

> dramatise but don't lie – don't ever lie

And 'spin'? Nothing more than putting the best slant on what you've got. Dramatise but don't lie. Don't ever lie. They won't believe you next time which is the problems all politicians have.

The tools of PR

- **Telling it as you'd like it heard**. The ability to create good, fact-based stories which say what the facts are, how it all happened, where and when, who did it and why and how much impact it's all going to have. Put in numbers. Put in facts.

● **Engaging attention**. Find 'hooks' or 'levers' that engage the poor, perspiring journalist you are sending this to. Something they don't know. Something that adds to what they do know. Something that is unexpected ('Onions are better than Viagra' – don't lie but you get my drift). Some unexpected benefit or something that refutes – strong if you have good facts – or builds on existing stories.

● **How to write a press release**. Press releases are a necessary evil which often get binned because they are boring and blatant pieces of selling. Five pieces of advice.

  ● Keep them brief and supported with good material – photographs, research, contacts.

  ● Get them to the right person – better still someone you know and are building a relationship with.

  ● If possible make them an exclusive – especially if it's an interesting story.

  ● See things from the journalist's viewpoint. They want to look good. Help him or her by giving them something which is new or edgy or funny or interesting, which may create a wave of interest. Do not be self-serving or boring.

  ● Local press want to fill their pages. Indulge this need by giving them great pictures and well-written material. They'll be grateful. A local slant is helpful.

● **Instant communication**. Email is the most exciting way of spreading news, fast and cheaply. E-letters can help you keep people up to date with what you are doing and be a great way of announcing things you want known. Blogs are a great way of stating positions, starting dialogue. Your customers are at it the whole time, often reviling you. Are you responding and on the case?

blogs are a great way of starting dialogue

● **The web**. Corporate web sites need constant updating and are usually a PR disaster – out of date and static. If you have one as a company or one yourself for your own company, update it every week. Better still appoint a 'site-minder' who at very low cost will stop you looking sloppy and out of touch. PR is about news and your web site is a news medium. News is now, not last week.

● **TV, radio, press interviews**. Do not be caught short. You need to have the confidence and the skills to do this. Two or three messages; good breathing techniques; looking the part (blue shirts on TV); being upbeat; recognising the interviewer wants 'good interview' not adversarial stuff, but not you doing a sales pitch either. If you try and do that you deserve to be beaten up. Anyone exposed to interviews needs training – a day with professionals will change your life. I can recommend the best: www.richardhall.biz.

● **The new PR tools**. PR is about more than the media. Increasingly, companies are using bespoke events to 'showcase' their clients' activities especially in Business to Business (B2B) – the sort of prestigious conference that people see value in attending.

● **Round tables**. Where groups of people share ideas, expertise and knowledge. Places where breakthrough thinking happens.

● **Workouts**. Where, a bit like town hall meetings, you assemble the people in the front line to meet and chew over how to improve a business issue. What you do with the outcome is the PR magic. Internal communications; external communications – there's something about engaging those in the front line that says you are honest about what you do. The guys who masterminded this technique working with General Electric, the massive US and global industrial and financial services conglomerate, are Robert H. Schaffer & Associates in the USA. www.rhsa.com.

- **Publications**. Don't be shy. If you have a great story to tell, print it, make it look important, publish and be praised.
- **Research**. Do it, use it. Anyone who has a product which they believe or know has functional or remedial effectiveness needs to get third-party research to prove it, and to publish it if it works out. The media love research. And so do I, because it should be hard to lie. Too many reputations are at stake. Research is about facts and in PR we like hard, shiny facts.

---

brilliant examples

- Heinz running a story based on research which got picked up by the *New Scientist*, the medical press and then ran in the *Mail*, among others, about the high levels of anti-carciogenic lycopene in Heinz Organic Tomato Ketchup.

- The Porsche garden at the Hampton Court Flower Festival 2008. Normally car manufacturers park their wretched car in front of a really dull flowerbed in a really dull garden reducing members of the RHS to spluttering rage. Porsche demonstrated their underground hydraulically operated garage complete with Porsche Carrera in a great town garden. A fun concept. And it all worked properly.

- In 2008 Orange gave tickets to the biggest gig of the year to people who donated just four hours of their time to volunteer work. What a brilliant double whammy – what a great story.

- Calvin Klein launched a fragrance called 'Secret Obsession' using actress Eva Mendes in the advertising in autumn of 2008. The commercial was a raunchy piece with an apparently naked Mendes writhing suggestively on a bed. And yes we do see one nipple. Briefly. The commercial was banned in the USA, leading to an outraged response from the client leading to the commercial appearing on

YouTube and then being removed from that to its reappearing on other sites with a volley of blogs saying 'show us that nipple'. It's a PR coup of massive proportions. I especially loved the chatroom comment, 'She's writhing around just as though she's got the most terrible cramp.'

---

brilliant tip

Oscar Wilde thought being in the news was brilliant. Brilliance lies in hitting headlines and controlling the news agenda. It lies in creating momentum and making your relations with the consumer very public. But the high-risk game you play is that it can all go very wrong.

Bad PR stories

> brilliance lies in creating momentum and making your relations with the consumer very public

You can get salmonella in your chocolate or the water you bottle can have benzene in it, or your crisps can be made from decomposed potatoes, or something worse can spin out of control. Losing control of the media is like having vertigo. Very frightening.

brilliant disasters

- Example: the **Galaxy** problem. A nice little poster for Galaxy ... which chunk of chocolate shall I have. Headline? *'Eeny meeny miny mo'*. No problem. Not brilliant – on the OK side of workmanlike. Until it fell into the spitting pit of damnation when someone in the press noted the next line was 'catch a nigger by his toe'.

● Example: when near facts become whole facts or suppositions become truths.

Fact: MMR jabs cause autism ... no they don't but ... (there's no smoke without a fire ... oh yes there is ... before the fire is lit).

Fact: plastic bags kill seabirds in their millions. No, plastic does but bags alone don't. But killer supermarket bags makes a better story than industrial waste.

Fact: imported flowers cause damaging carbon emissions through being flown in big planes ... er ... truer fact – heated greenhouses growing flowers nearer home does much worse damage.

Advertising and PR are both about stories

The best ad man became one of the best PR men – Lord Tim Bell. He understands better than most the role intelligent PR brings to bear. Here's what his company's web site says:

'In today's media-led environment, brand awareness and recall are only vague indicators of how a company's marketing is performing; brand reputation is the measure that truly matters.'

(Chime Communications).

The PR business still has more than its fill of leggie lovelies – but nowadays they also tend to have firsts and 2.1s from Oxbridge. And the sector works harder and more intelligently than it ever used to. If advertising was an inspiration business, PR tended to be a perspiration business. Now it's a bit of both.

Brilliant PR is about two things

Having a strong sense of the zeitgeist surrounding a product or a market.

The ability to be a compelling story creator and story-teller.

Summary

1 **The PR ideas**

A brilliant PR idea gives the media a newsy story they can use, consumers something they enjoy and staff a level of satisfaction and fun. It's achieved by a combination of creativity (the wow factor), connectivity (knowing the right people to get the job done and talked about), hard work (motivated staff working their asses off) and luck (nothing in PR is guaranteed – you just minimise the chances of it going wrong).

2 **The human qualities**

Brilliance in PR is about having a series of qualities.

- Knowing exactly how you want to be seen.
- Having great antennae and knowing exactly where danger and opportunity lie.
- Having a nose for a good meaty story – one that journalists want to write – one which gives them a real sense of drama, human interest and news.
- Being a great persistent salesman with very thick skin.
- Knowing how to stay on message without being boring.
- Being totally clear about what is a story and what is not.
- Having vast energy.

3 **Engagement**

Loving your client . . . well not loving them perhaps but wanting – achingly – to see them do incredibly well. I have never come across anyone any good in marketing services who didn't want their client and their brand to win – not for the money but because winning is what they felt they deserved.

CHAPTER 9

Sponsorship – living close to excitement

How sponsorship works

You pay money to own (or co-own) the rights to a player, car, horse, event, series or whatever. Theoretically you could sponsor almost anything. And when you get sponsorship right it can work incredibly well for you. You get the association of being linked to a winner and if you are lucky you may have a wonderful brand ambassador. The John Player Special Formula One Sponsorship was an example of rare brilliance where the car was the cigarette pack and Ayrton Senna, the charismatic driver, was a winner.

> **brilliant tip**
>
> When and if you have decided to get involved in sponsorship, as a rule of thumb expect to double the cost of getting sponsorship rights on marketing the fact you are doing it. Unless you fully exploit the rights you shouldn't be involved in sponsorship.

What has changed?

Sponsorship is economy-dependent. It's much more likely to be used widely in the good times rather than the not so good times. In Europe alone, the Financial Services business spent nearly $7 billion in 2007 on sponsoring sport. Any guesses as to what the spend will be in 2009 or 2010?

Sponsorship is very big business. But some heavy hitters are questioning the real value of big time sponsorship. Here's what Antonio Perez, CEO of Kodak, had to say about the Olympics:

'The Olympics has become too political and divisive for most major brands to continue to support with large sponsorships.'

But not all sponsorship is hugely expensive – especially if it's local or niche.

Sometimes putting money into, say, a golf event and entertaining your golf-loving customers can pay dividends. Getting to spend hours of quality time with important customers for your product and services may become a really sensible investment. So too may an investment in a cause-related event in motivating young talent in your business or younger customers whom you discover are very concerned about certain issues. This is about knowing your customers, what they think and targeting them.

> your job is to sell more of your product at the lowest possible cost

In general avoid controversy. Avoid people who are on a mission to convert. Your job is to sell more of your product at the lowest possible cost, not to put your company's money to charitable ends.

But if you are going to sponsor a charity, check them out through the Charity Commission, speak to other sponsors, meet (insist on meeting) their CEO and Chair of Trustees. Judge whether they could speak winningly, convincingly and amusingly to your key customers. Study their accounts. Judge how important you'd be to them.

brilliant disaster

Beware the wrong association

I was driving through Brighton when I saw a sign for the Brighton Trades and Labour Union set somewhat crookedly on a rundown building on the A270. It was, I saw, endorsed, sponsored or at any rate the sign was paid for by Foster's Lager. Why? What on earth did they see themselves getting from this?

brilliant example

But seek the one that genuinely makes a difference

The dollars going into sponsorship says when it works. In Dubai the new Dubai Metro is calling for sponsors. And why not? When sponsorship works it works big time. So the Emirates stadium at Arsenal seems a great piece of branding as does the O2 Stadium (aka 'the Dome'). It's now the most successful entertainment venue in the world.

Why some companies get into sponsorship

The trouble is too many sponsorship decisions are made at Chairman or CEO level, leaving the poor marketing people to sweep up the debris of a glamorous dinner party conversation which led to a good-idea-at-the-time investment decision, but is simply not properly thought through and evaluated. If this has happened you have little choice but to make the best of it and whatever you do, try to ensure you merchandise the sponsorship brilliantly. And do the following:

● Make it look as though it's thought through (sometimes

'*post rationalisation*' is the most valuable marketing tool in a company you can have).

- Make sure the sponsored body, event or whatever/whoever becomes very visible and appealing to staff and their families – this is called doing what Barack Obama did – growing a huge '*sales-force*'.

- Make it seem fun and involving to all your major stakeholders – suppliers, customers, local media. This is called '*warming-up*' the key opinion makers.

If you can't remember the sponsor or the association who wins?

Who sponsors the Premier League? You have two seconds to answer this question.

Which of the following are sponsors for which Premier Division Football Clubs?

- Samsung
- Thomas Cook
- Emirates
- Garmin
- Acorns
- Crown Paints
- Karoo
- OKI
- Chang Beer
- Boyle

You have five minutes to answer and you can then call a friend.

The point I am making is these are in general pretty low profile companies and I wonder if some of them really make their sponsorship work.

Making it work for you

The lesson here is what does each sponsor do with their sponsorship? Britannia Building Society sensibly sponsor neighbouring Stoke City. And I suspect OKI use the wit and nous of Lucius Peart and his very astute team of marketers to charm the socks off a relatively small number of B2B customers at Portsmouth. Being flattered by the successful, rich and famous can move mountains – *'Peter Crouch, come over here, son, and say hallo to this nice client of our sponsor.'*

Sponsorship checklist

General questions

1   What is the key marketing issue you are seeking to solve? Is it brand awareness? Is it product knowledge? Is it about warding off competition? Is it about making your brand, product or company seem more important than it is – rather like the Avis – a 'we try harder' strategy? Is it a consumer or a trade issue? Do you have a problem with your relationship with the trade or your suppliers? Is it a global, national or local issue? Be clear about all of this first.

2   Why are you thinking about sponsorship?

3   When you evaluate the option in terms of ticking off the following does it still make sense? Appeals to target market; appeals to trade customers; appeals to staff; compares well in cost terms with other options in terms of cost per person reached and in terms of influence and impact. Be ruthless in evaluating the cost-effectiveness.

4   How much is the most you can afford to invest? Sponsorship can be very expensive. Be careful. And

remember you need to double the sponsorship cost to cover the marketing of it. And then you may need more to make it really swing. This is expensive but can be very rewarding work. Be careful you don't assume you can get away with a smaller budget than normal. That's like buying an air ticket halfway to New York.

Specific questions

And now there are some questions anyone potentially involved in sponsorship should ask.

- Is this association going to improve the reputation of your brand overall?

- Where is this going to have the biggest impact (quantify this) and the least impact (why?)?

- Is the sponsorship in line with your strategy?

- What ideas do you have that will make this sponsorship really different, special and exciting?

- Is there any danger of the sponsorship being more to the advantage of what you are sponsoring than to you the sponsor?

- You probably need to employ someone to champion the sponsorship with very clear rules set by you. Have you costed this in?

- Even so it will take your time too. How much time are you prepared to invest?

- Can you get good media coverage from this? How do you know?

- Will you be very hard-nosed in seeing how you can maximise the benefits of a sponsorship? And very clear about the personalities of the people you are sponsoring – are they likely to be wonderful brand ambassadors? Are they winners?

Good luck. Answer all these questions honestly and you will make a better decision and even arrange a brilliant sponsorship.

brilliant tip

Make your story an exciting one and the media will follow you. Just being there isn't enough. You have to milk it. You have to be creative and engaging.

Sponsorship is expensive. Think hard before getting involved in something which takes your time and gives back less than it should. Most sponsorships that are disappointing are like that because no one admits or knows how much commitment successful sponsorship requires.

brilliant example

What's really hard to do? Sail solo (been done). And do it round the world (been done and done). As a woman (been done). Going round the *wrong* way (not been done – are you crazy? – what sort of woman would do that?). Meet the glamorous and intelligent Dee Caffari who as I write is about to compete in the Vendee race.

Sarah Loghran at Aviva, her sponsor, says:

'Dee is an attractive, inspirational character who is an excellent communicator and has become a real brand ambassador for us.'
And yes she *is* attractive.

A series of factors combine to make a sponsorship brilliant. Middlesex Cricket Club have as their main sponsor Northern Rock. Not so brilliant. They have subsidiary sponsors, six of them – Catlin, Vauxhall, Clydesdale, Aegon, Fitzgerald and Law and Breakthrough Breast Cancer. The team wears pink shirts in support of the charity in one-day matches and 20:20 games. Now that is brilliant.

It was Karen Earl, Chair of the European Sponsorship Association, who said:

'Sport is extremely engaging and it can give a human face to industry.'

No more so than in Rugby where Brains Beer have renewed their sponsorship with the Welsh Rugby Union Team. So far so good but it's rendered brilliant for all concerned by the very close interest, support and participation the team gets from Katherine Jenkins and Charlotte Church. Brilliant as a sexy and relevant package. Very Welsh; very much a 'welcome in the hillside'.

Hot air ballooning to those who've done it is a magical experience with lots of opportunity to do big branding. Thus Lurpak Light sponsored and broke the record for the highest man has gone suspended by toy balloons accompanied by the big Lurpak hot air balloon. The lovely Ian Ashpole of Flying Pictures did this. It was on the front page of every paper the next day and ITV that night. That's when sponsorship comes into its own.

Summary

Sponsorship is one of the early casualties in a budget cut (witness Honda and Formula One), so make sure the economic case for doing it is cast iron.

Do not just be taken in by an opportunity to associate yourself with your favourite sport or charity. Remember they want your money. Remember you want sales.

If you do decide for good cost reasons to do it, one of which may be that this will increase your opportunities to develop your business relationship with some major customers, then that's a justification to go ahead, but whether it's a big or a small sponsorship ensure that you maximise:

● Your branding

● Your importance to the sponsor's marketing

● Use of and exploitation rights of their key players – players

and management (make your continued sponsorship
conditional on this being properly fulfilled)

● The guaranteed engagement of the sponsor with a lot of
   people in your company

● Frequent (monthly) reviews of activity and their effect on
   your business – do not let this sponsorship slide down your
   'Really Important Agenda'

● Be determined and insistent you get value for money and
   that there is no sign of the sponsored activity slipping
   backwards in their focus on their sponsor.

*In my experience sponsorship is often a decision lightly taken and
poorly seen through. Do not underestimate how much of your time it
will take. But if you want to do it and
can justify it on cost and impact
grounds then really go for it – hard
work and good humour will see you
through.*

> sponsorship ... do not
> underestimate how
> much of your time it will
> take

CHAPTER 10

Design is it!

How design works

Tom Peters said, 'Design is it!' To many of us the importance of design has never been greater. However good the marketing may be, if the product or service doesn't look great you will always struggle. That's why Absolut Vodka is such a marketing gift. What a bottle. What a delight. Ditto Ben & Jerry's. Ditto Innocent and so on ... I am going to consider how to attune yourselves better to product design and packaging design in the next few pages.

brilliant tip

The brilliance of design lies not just in the end product, it also lies in the process of working out what the real task is.

'What you need to know about a problem only becomes apparent as you are trying to solve it.'

(Richard McCormack of RJM Design, Cambridge)

So let's start with the brief.

Design brief

I have already shown the form of briefing I use. The brief is the tool that allows us to wrestle with the

innovation is at the heart of brilliance in design, marketing and business challenge which in turn leads to innovation. It's innovation that is at the heart of brilliance in design, marketing and business.

Here's what I'd add to that for a product brief and a packaging brief:

Product

● What do I want my product to do that is different from what is already on the market?

● How do I want the consumer to feel about this product?

● How modern or how traditional do I want it to seem – leading edge or trailing edge?

● Do I want it to be multifunctional or focused on one key asset?

● How do I want to achieve a worried 'oh, my goodness!' from my competitors?

● How important is look as opposed to function (example: think round tea bags, think Bose sound systems, think Bickerton Bicycles).

Packaging

● How visible does it need to be – line up all competitive packs (for a breakthrough example look at [yellow tail] outer packs – real stand-out).

● How can you 'own' colour – the Heinz 'turquoise' is protected by trademark.

● How can you improve the information and copy on your pack? Obviously by getting professional help from a sign expert. But also by deciding:

  – what must be on there

  – what would be very helpful to have on there

  – what would be nice to have on there.

● Remember that packaging is about more than function. It is the 'face' a consumer or customer sees first and as we are constantly told – it's also true – first impressions count.

we are constantly told – it's also true – first impressions count

- In retail we are told research shows as much as 75 per cent of purchases are made on impulse. I actually doubt that statistic, but why run the risk? Be brighter, more interesting, sharper and better on display. Whatever else do not be eclipsed by your competitors. Be the one that is outstanding.

- For help contact the Design Council – www.designcouncil.org.uk. – read *Design Week* – www.designweek.co.uk – and talk to people who've had design teams working with them, so you can get a feel for who's hot or not. And if you need a low cost local operation, very often they'll be excellent, look up Design Consultants, Design – Advertising and Graphic, Design – Product under www.yell.com. There are 160 listed, for instance, in Brighton. Look to see what they've done and what you like. Create a shortlist and ask to see more of their work.

What has changed?

We have realised that how well we make things look – from the appearance to the pack design to the ambience in which we buy the product – actually make a difference. In the past, many people in marketing had slunk past the design issue – no longer. What things look like, feel like and smell like are all critical.

Design differentiates

John Deere have it spot on. John Deere is the most stolen tractor in the UK. Villains are queuing up to nick the green and yellow darlings. Ask them and they'll tell you, 'It's the bleeding design,

son, innit?' John Deere has the same charisma as Porsche and
Bose. Exclusive but not excluding. Henry Dreyfus, the great
American designer – he made everyday things look good, easy to
use and unobtrusive – appears in their ads and what a great line
they have about him:

'Say the name and every industrial designer in the world genuflects.'

Design is an amazing component in marketing.

---

design is an amazing
component in marketing

Ask people why they buy Nike . . . or
Apple . . . or Sony . . . or Prada? Why
is Ben & Jerry's packaging so great?
Sit and look at it. Look really hard.
I'll give you a few tips.

- Font
- Colours
- Authenticity of handwriting
- Product descriptors
- Simplicity

Design can make you fall in love

Tom Peters, to whom design is so important, shows why it is he
gets quite worked up about Stanley.

*'I love . . . L-O-V-E . . . my Stanley hammers. And $2.6billion in
sales says I'm not alone. Like Nike, the functionality is . . . great.
And so are the aesthetics . . . by design.'*

Spotting and understanding great design

Some people 'get' design, and some don't, but just for a moment
reflect on the unutterable joy a 'just-right' design has.

- Look at the new Boeing 787 Dreamliner and see how
  glorious a plane can look.

- The Mazda MX-5 borrowing from the old sports car character of the MG and translating this into the late twentieth century had a similar effect on one's mind.

- As does virtually everything Dyson does, but especially the Airblade hand dryer. How can the process of going to a public loo be made so much more pleasurable? These things look great, they are very fast, very hygienic, cost-efficient (they tell me) and energy-efficient. They are brilliantly designed.

- The DreamWorks logo is perfect.

- Montblanc. The ultimate in pens. Very black and very shiny and wonderful. Just brilliant.

What great design does is fizz. It stands you apart from other stuff. It does half the marketing job just by being what it is. In their super book about design, *A Smile in the Mind*, Beryl McAlhone and David Stuart argue that graphics are made memorable by using witty thinking. What's more, ideas that happen in the mind, stay in the mind. And I love this.

So what do you do?

If you are launching your own brand, have no money and are very brave then you can do it all yourself, but be bold; speak from the heart; remember – you have to live with this.

And then there are just three things:

i) decide, define and brief what you want your brand to look and feel like

ii) find other examples of what you want your design to resemble but not copy

iii) don't be afraid to reject what you or your designers come up with . . . it's easier to say 'no' now than it is later.

- The Shell logo
- The 1972 Penguin paperback for *Billy Liar* – based on the Woodbine cigarette packet design
- I ♥ New York
- Harvey Nichols' Traditional Christmas Pudding with the wrapping in the design of a large sixpence
- The Jif Lemon packaging
- You learn how to be discerning about great design by looking at great pack designs (Heinz, Kellogg's, Innocent) or bottles (Absolut, Antiquary) or cover designs for books or products (Apple anything, Bose, Wedgwood). Eventually pennies begin to drop.
- As with so much in marketing, you need to be able to be ahead of the curve. Designer Dewys Lasdon said:

'Our job is to give the client what he never dreamed he wanted.'

Designed to succeed

If you think about the most successful products, how they look is often key to their success, but increasingly what is happening is a rejection of over-design especially when it comes to packaging.

From being a peripheral discipline design has leapt to the centre of the marketing stage. A TV is not just a machine on which to look at programmes. It's important focal point in a living room. It's a piece of furniture. A car (unless you are Jeremy Clarkson) is not a virility symbol or high performance machine – so out of date that – but a statement about the new you. Look at the design of the Mercedes A6 or the Toyota Prius. Take another look at the Mazda M5 and the Ford Ka. Then take a look at

Apple. Talk about love affairs because, like Stanley, this is what that brand's design inspires. And in the very dead of night you'll hear a John Deere starting up in deepest Essex hopefully to the declamation, 'You're nicked, son.'

Truly design is it!

> design has leapt to the centre of the marketing stage

CHAPTER 11

Direct marketing – the world of measuring results

How direct marketing works

Direct marketing is about directly marketing to people on a one-to-one basis. It depends on creating and being able to process data so you can personalise your messaging to your audience in the most effective and economic way. At its simplest, direct marketing involves sending people coupons with offers (as Direct Line do), sending letters (often called junk mail), doing telesales and at its most sophisticated managing e-commerce programmes through web sites (like Tesco or Amazon). Direct marketing became highly favoured by clients in the 1980s because it is so clearly measurable – you do x, you get y responses, sales increase by z; cost of x minus margin on z = profit.

brilliant tip

Your database is your radar system. And of course the old-fashioned marketers just had grapeshot and prayer to rely on. You now have the same sort of equipment as a brain surgeon so you can and you should really get inside the minds of your precious customers and see how to help make them do what you want.

What has changed?

There are some talented direct marketers around like Terry Hunt of Evans Hunt Scott and Stan Rapp formerly of Rapp and Collins. I thought Stan, whom I met once, was an engaging and sharp thinker and must be sunning himself on a well-deserved yacht or whatever. But no. In *Marketing Conversations* lead story, 29 August 2007 quoted from the *New York Times*, who must have seen this as big news, it said:

'Stan Rapp, an 82-year-old veteran of direct marketing, is teaming up with Halyard Capital to create Engauge, a combination of agencies in various fields. Engauge is hoping to become a company that combines data analysis, behavioural targeting and direct marking to provide marketer results they can truly "gauge".'

And this is what I love about the Americans – they never stop. So the pioneering force in 1980s marketing (direct marketing) has joined up with the new kid on the block in 2008 (digital marketing) which everybody believes will shape the future of marketing. And it must be a mighty powerful concept to get an 82-year-old to take notice and risk his fortune. And we see that 'measurement' has now become 'gauge', an altogether more sophisticated concept. Gauge is active measurement – measurement you do something with.

How direct marketing broke through

When he was young (a mere 61) Stan said in his book *MaxiMarketing* published in 1987:

The fascination with 'creative' advertising is giving way to a concern for accountability and responsiveness.

He observed the disintegration of homogeneous consumer

groups and the remorseless progress from mass marketing to segmented marketing to niche marketing to one-to-one marketing.

And now we have the tools to reach small groups or even individuals cheaply. In 1973 it cost over $7 to access 1000 bits of information. Today it is virtually free. (Although Stan was wrong about creative advertising. Some 21 years later the fascination for it remains.)

We are in a new phase of marketing which is virtually 'customised'. So you order your own customised Toyota, BMW Mini, your self-designed Nike shoe online. Try it, it's magic. Direct marketing comes into its own. The ultimate consequence is interesting. Thus in *Beverage Digest* quoted in the *New York Times* in 1985, Jesse Meyers said, 'The more products you can go to market with the more constituencies you can attract.'

So modern business can do what we when young could only dream about. This is à la carte plus. And what makes sense is the argument that well-managed databases allow you to have better and more fruitful conversations with your customers and that must make good, sound commercial sense.

The key rules of direct marketing

1 Understand the power of building a database which defines your customer by frequency of purchase, where they live, how much they spend and so on, and so on. As much information as you can get, so when you talk to them you sound as though you know them . . . which do you prefer 'Dear Richard' or 'Dear Customer'?

2 Understand the general arithmetic of direct marketing: 95 per cent of letters that are not individually addressed get no response, 93 per cent of letters that are individually addressed get no response and that 40 per cent of all letters

sent out don't even get looked at let alone read – straight in the bin. So you have to create a lot of activity to make a few sales: 1000 letters might get 70 responses which might convert to 10 sales in the very end.

3 Understand the long game. Marketing today is about building relationships. We've heard of the 'lifetime customer' – the person who spends £20 a month with you will spend nearly £10,000 over 40 years – if you keep them. The intimacy of the narrowcast direct marketing relationship enables you to achieve what a broadcast medium can't. Don't think of one or two mailings think of a long programme.

4 Study the direct marketing geniuses like Direct Line. What they discovered was that this was a game of scale and of quantity, not a few quality big hits. Direct Motor Insurance accounts for 60 per cent of sales in the UK in just 20+ years and Direct Line were the force that did it. Catchy ads, a promise of value, a brilliantly run call centre, a brilliant proposition. Try and meet anyone who's worked there and talk to them.

5 Become a flexible measuring machine. Measure the effect of every ad, of every activity, of everything you do. Discard what doesn't work. Retain what does. This is like fishing. Judge your success by how many fish you catch, not how pretty your flies are.

6 You don't have to be crass to win. Someone said to me, 'I hate this junk mail – I'd rather be poor than do it.' As ever, be true to your brand. The material produced by Johnny Boden, Charles Tyrwhitt and the White Company are fabulous.

7 Getting started means you need to talk to experts. Always talk to experts otherwise you'll end up creating a square

wheel. Experts cost money unless they are the Royal Mail, who know more about this subject than anyone in the world – contact thelab@royalmail.com or stan.kozlowski@ royalmail.com. Best to call Antony Miller at their Mail Media Centre in Stukeley Street, London WC1V 7AB, 020 7421 2251. You should also talk to Yell, www.yellgroup.com.

8 Talking to experts is always smart. Try the Institute of Direct Marketing. www.idm.com. Read anything by Drayton Bird, Alan Tapp, Bob Stone or Stan Rapp.

9 If you can't afford to use professionals what comes next is critical. If you can afford professionals it's just very important. Decide on your tone

> this is your brand, not a sales or corporate voice, be you

of voice. This is you talking in print or via a call centre to your customers and prospects. This is your brand, not a sales or corporate voice. Be you.

10 We all do direct marketing all the time. In the emails we send. In the letters we write. In the phone calls we make. It's time to reflect on how we can all make a more telling impression. For instance, have you thought of measuring how effective you are? The 'creativity' that Stan Rapp put in inverted commas is actually the stuff that makes people stop, look and smile and that has generally been absent from direct marketing. The practice has more often resembled Meccano than magic. So be magic and try to be more exciting and stand out from the rest.

The current huge opportunity for direct marketing

If direct marketing fails to understand how to charm, engage and seduce rather than just sell loudly (and there are exceptions) then there is a solution.

Do it better.

Imagine a world where direct marketing was always witty, fresh and exciting. Imagine briefing your direct marketing people to produce material that was riveting not just efficient. Remember this is no longer megaphone country; this is quite an intimate one-to-one conversation. Imagine having a drink with a friend; telling jokes; telling stories; not talking too loudly; not showing off and selling but giving the person you are talking to the chance to talk back to you.

always keep your communications fresh

So is this soft sell? Softer – yes – and more in tune with what we know people want. Be persistent of course, but sensitive in talking to your customer base. The new way forward is in telling them new things; telling them about deals. And not boringly telling them the same thing. One rule shines through which is always keep your communications fresh.

Dull direct marketing may be measurable but that doesn't mean in the long run that's all that matters.

How very good it gets

 **examples**

Tesco online beats the rest

Waitrose, who are super in almost every respect, couldn't understand why I was convulsed with laughter when I ordered wine online from them and when I phoned about delivery said they couldn't give me a delivery slot – no not even a day, let alone am or pm, while Tesco have got it down to slots of two hours. When I told them about Tesco they didn't believe me, didn't think it possible.

Tesco know more about me than is probably healthy. They know I buy a lot of wine.

Their web site is terrific. Buying is easy. Fulfilment is spectacular. They have changed part of my life ... for the better.

Tesco is the most successful, intelligent and profitable online grocer and it deserves to be.

Buying books in the small hours

It's midnight or beyond. Everyone's asleep. I'm sitting at my PC clearing up emails. I suddenly remember the name of a book recommended to me – *Alpha Dogs* by James Harding – I must have it. On to Amazon. Ho, ho ... £7 off. And while I'm here ... £100 later I press 'place order' and two days later the books I ordered arrive.

This is the best thing ever. They even gift wrap the Christmas presents I send without my having to even touch them myself. Amazon is a customer service triumph and very impressive in every respect.

It took its founder Jeff Bezos, former investment banker, nearly ten years to get it into profit and this included surviving the dot.com bubble burst of 2001. From books to CDs, video games and now in Mercer Island, Washington, Seattle – Amazon Fresh – a grocery service.

Are they the only people who through intelligent data management manage to cross-sell so well?

The best hi-fi I know

They have a great marketing presence. They constantly mail me and do it well. They have their top-of-the-range gear in the best shops. They have a trophy outlet in Regent's Street. They have a functional, slightly clunky web site. But Bose are the business.

Here's what Peter G., a sound engineer, is quoted as saying.

'I like it here because we are not in some back room with a bunch of CAD machines pumping out stuff and throwing it over the wall to production. It's much more of an interactive environment with really talented engineers from all parts of the company.'

I believe Peter G. because I believe in this 44-year-old company, whose technology is impressive, the product sounds good and like an Aga it's very simple to use.

Most of all I like the fact it's so easy to buy their products. And the fact they keep me very Bose-conscious about deals or new developments.

 **brilliant** tip

Be generous. Be kinder to your converts and to your existing consumers than to those you are trying to convert.

Summary

● **You can measure if it's working**. Direct marketing finds favour rightly because you can actually 'gauge' how it is working. This makes ROI so much easier. This is marketing that accountants like.

● **You can target consumers very specifically**. Modern technology allows us to slice and dice data so we can build hugely complex but useful consumer profiles and models. This allows us, in theory, to spend our money much more effectively only talking to the people we want to talk to and saying to each of them the sort of things they want to hear.

● **Integrated marketing is a buzz phrase**. Direct marketing as we can see in the alliance of direct and digital can be a key component in integrated marketing. But the real key is getting closer and closer to your customer.

● **Creativity sells**. The trouble is the people who do direct marketing tend not to be focused on the quality of the creativity in their messaging, which is often dull because they are more into the maths of the subject than the fun of seduction.

● **This represents a huge opportunity**. Put wit, freshness and vitality into the communication and something special could emerge. Just because you can be measured doesn't mean you have to be dull.

> just because you can be measured doesn't mean you have to be dull

- **Sing better**. Bad direct marketing is often just bad customer management. But when it sings – like Tesco and Amazon and Bose – it sings.

CHAPTER 12

Customer relations marketing – the people side of marketing

How CRM works

'm not yet quite blue in the face saying that it's getting the people thing right that will get you marketing brilliance faster than anything else. You've got to hire the right people, work with the right people, learn how to talk to people, enjoy people, respect people, love people. Most of all you've got to love your customers.

you've got to love your customers

First impressions count. Walk into the reception of any company and the kind of greeting you get and the noise of energy levels you are subject to tell you a lot about the company and the brand. People at work and on display are the brand.

Brilliant first impressions

When Saatchi & Saatchi first set up in business in the early 1970s in Golden Square in Soho their reception was about half the floor space of the whole agency. The back offices were small but the first impressions were of a big and successful business.

Go into Abbott Mead Vickers, Marylebone Road, and you get a feeling of freedom, youth and of a lot of business going on.

ING headquarters in Amsterdam is a magnificent trophy building designed like a huge glass boat on stilts. The offices inside are full of trees and gardens. More flora than people. This is business as I'd like it to be – full of good thoughtful people doing good work. And this is a bank.

The Royal Mail Media Centre in Holborn feels alive, modern and buzzy.

Google HQ in Zurich is colourful, fun, witty and lively. A great sense of helping people be at their best and everywhere huge pride in the brand. There is a real sense of focus and teamwork. And how about reclaimed and brightly painted cable cars as breakout rooms?

brilliant disaster

And one not so brilliant first impression. A digital marketing company I saw recently had shared offices with no one on reception so I wandered around for a while until someone said, 'Who are you looking for?' I rather felt like saying, 'Don't bother I'm a virtual guest'.

People as brands

We need to personalise the whole branding thing, which can be very powerful. The killer question which can be asked of yourself or your company is this:

'Who are you (now)?'

So – go on – ask it. Not who were you or who would you like to be – who are you NOW?

Jesper Kunde, the Danish marketer and author of *Corporate Religion: Building a Strong Company*, says this:

'Branding is about the company fulfilling its potential, not about a new logo. What is my mission in life? What do I want to convey to people? And how do I make sure that what I have to offer the world is actually unique?'

And interestingly, people are unique, but in large companies we seem determined to train them into clones and thereby make the businesses similar, which is really stupid. Which is why Innocent, now, or the maverick advertising agency FCO, a decade or so back, were so unique. They were different.

Look at the big people brands of the past ten years. Bill Clinton. Tony Blair. Kylie Minogue. Eddie Murphy. The late Anita Roddick. Richard Branson. Steve Jobs. Jamie Oliver. Carla Sarkozy. Madonna. Helen Mirren. Shane Warne and so on . . . All of these stand or stood for something. Linda Barker thinks she is a brand and describes herself in the third person which is a bit weird as I remarked to Richard Hall just the other day. Anita Roddick was a remarkable force who seamlessly stood for Body Shop and it stood for her, as did Laura Ashley (who died tragically in 1985) with her chain of stores.

In politics the personality of the candidate plays a major part – does the camera love them? Do they have smiling eyes? Do they look honest? Politics plays out on TV mainly and Tony Blair had the touch (not so much latterly) as did Paddy Ashdown as did Ken Clarke as did Dennis Healey – that deeply clever and funny man.

How to improve your relationship with customers

1 **Hire the right people**. When you hire people think of yourself as a casting director. Your corporate brand needs a mix of talent, not just one sort of person. But if they don't fit in don't hire them, however great their CV. At Google they interview everyone 20 times – just to make sure.

2 **Be what you are**. Help your people play to their strengths,

which is what brands do. Ben & Jerry's doesn't waste its time talking about its slimming credentials. It lives in the land of Yum. Make sure everyone is clear about what you stand for in simple English.

3 **Hire a great receptionist**. It's a really important job. The signpost to a company.

4 **Learn how to smile**. You could try practising. Smiling is an art not an occasional habit.

5 **Create an office that stands for your brand**. Decoratively and in terms of layout. Encourage people to make where they work stand for your brand values which they are trying to promote.

> if you remember your customers' names they'll remember you

6 **Remember people's names**. This is something everyone in a business needs to do effortlessly. If you remember your customers' names they'll remember you.

7 **Measure your performance**. Meet all your customers once or twice a year and get them to tell you how you score along a whole variety of axes including the following:

● Efficiency

● Effectiveness

● Improvement (or reverse) overall

● Customer service

● Are you made to feel welcome?

● And appreciated?

● Overall how satisfied are you with the service you get?

You can do this as an email check using say a six-point scale (0 = terrible; 6 = brilliant) but you need to follow it up with a one-to-one conversation as well, so that you can say 'thank you', or make immediate changes that are needed;

and so you can read between the lines, which is often where the most interesting information is hidden.

8 **Training**. Money spent ensuring you constantly train your people (and yourself) to be better at customer relationships will not be money wasted. Like presentation skills it's all too often taken for granted.

Customer service. Be a brand warrior not a brand wimp

Rule number one: you cannot hope to be brilliant at marketing if you don't deliver brilliant customer service.

They say that in the US customer service tends to be a bit cold, but always delivered with a smile, while in the UK it tends to be tepid with a frown although it's getting better mainly because of the influx of graduate ambitious-minded foreigners.

Fact: the eastern Europeans and the Germans are really good at this, as are the French when on song and in love with life.

Fact: you get out of life what you put in. Being great at customer service is one of the best and most fun jobs there is. The brand warriors fight their way to the front trying to outperform their peers at exceeding customer expectation.

Fact: serving customers is what generates trust and money.

Fact: the warriors in this marketing war are going to be mostly in customer service. This is how brands can distinguish themselves by the quantity of goodwill they bring to their consumers.

 **tip**

If you genuinely don't LOVE your customers how on earth do you expect them to LOVE you and your brand?

Keeping them, not just winning them

The art of keeping your customers is underestimated:

- it isn't easy in a competitive world;
- keeping them costs a fraction of the cost of winning new customers;
- keeping them doesn't seem as sexy as winning new ones but it's your number one need in building a sustainable business.

I've used this statement so many times, but as you'll be discovering, one of the weapons of brilliant marketing is repetition. One of the weapons of brilliant marketing is repetition. Charles Orvis said (and it's so good I've quoted it twice in this book):

'Your customer's right even when he's goddamned wrong.'

CHAPTER 13

Experiential
marketing –
using the
senses to
market
yourself

How experiential marketing works

I t does what it says ... it plays with the senses. It's been happening now for years but it used to be more prosaic. It was called merchandising and romancing a product. Now it's a science and serious. It asks the question – how can you dramatise a brand sensually so it speaks more loudly, much more excitingly and illustrates all its attributes?

Imagine the future

How can you activate consumer reactions positively? Imagine the smell of baby powder, the sound of a baby gurgling, films of babies being shown, the touch of really soft towelling, a kitchen with new baby foods, new baby toys everywhere, touch-screens to check out anything new about babies and a celebratory glass of bubbly to round off the whole experience. This is a prime-site Mothercare of the future or if not them then Autour de Bébé. This is theatre where the customer experience is raised to a very high level of interest and expectation.

What has changed

1   **The need for something different** which distinguishes a brand and gives it real cut through in a retail environment.

What most marketers are currently doing would have been OK in the distant past but now we live in much more discriminating times. Technology, film, video games have heightened the point at which our senses respond in a retail environment.

2 **Retail is more than a warehouse experience**.
   Technology has moved on so fast we really can create virtual reality situations. Very few of the obstacles that once stopped us doing convincing experiential marketing exist any more. We can do theatre now and should. Shoppers need bargain basements for sure, but they sometimes need to be wooed a bit and wooed a bit cleverly. Theme parks and Disney especially have primed our market to expect more. But we as marketers need to expect more too. We are not just there to sell stuff. We are also there to astonish and delight.

> shoppers need to be
> wooed a bit cleverly

3 **Premium brands need lavish love.** In the spoil-yourself world of expensive cost-more-than-they're-intrinsically-worth mega brands, as well as almost everywhere in the great New York stores, the experience is phenomenal. Understand how to create this and understand branding at its highest level.

A sensual adventure – which teaches you a lot

Let me take you on a short journey, a journey through some of the most wonderful department stores and shops in the world. I'll keep it brief but share with me the 'rush' of excitement a great shopper experience and brilliant experiential marketing can deliver. Consider how you'd manage to create something as exciting that exploited all the senses.

● **La Fromagerie, Moxon Street, Marylebone**. It just

smells wonderful. The shop itself is contained within a mini Dean & DeLuca type grocery outlet which has a long, shared table in their tasting café. Sacks of succulent, speciality potatoes lie rumpled on the floor. It's a world of quiche and sun-dried aubergine. It creates a brilliant appetising show. First and last this is a cheese shop. The 'cheese room' is an amazing blend of exotic products. A cornucopia of smelly delight.

- **Clarins in Selfridges**. Actually the whole store owes more to the world of magicians and caves of treasure than it does to retailing. Its ethos is indulgence, and they are indulging millions of pounds to make their point. It's pure theatre. It's credo is indulgence. But Clarins is a laboratory of expertise an anti-ageing elixirs 'womanned' by smart bright people. It lives and speaks knowledge of the skin.

- **Daunts Bookshop**. In Marylebone. It's a beautiful building with a galleried interior where at the back they segregate books by country so en route to say Syria you'd be able to equip yourself with a where-to-eat book, a travel guide, a novel, a recipe book and some translated Syrian poems say. It smells of reading and a love of books. It is full of experience.

- **Experiential for pets**. A German pet food company, Affinity Petcare, had posters which said 'listen to your nose' at pet height. Behind the posters they place fresh pet food, the smell of which was emitted through small holes. Lots of dogs. Lots of interested owners. Lots of experience.

- **The one that got away**. It was to have been the 'Whisky Dome' for a well-known brand. But they had a budget cut. It was a mobile sampling station comprising an inflatable dome which when you went in rocked all the senses. Sight. On all walls great film of Scotland – deer, pheasant, waterfalls, glens. Sight. Beautiful kilted girls serving the amber nectar (sorry Foster's.) Sound. Bagpipes in the background. The cry of curlews. Smell. The smell of heather wafted through. The smell of fresh air, a constant breeze – important in an inflatable dome. Taste. Well obviously the whisky. Touch. Everything very soft or very hard. Lumps of granite. Hard tables. Soft grassy carpeting. It'll happen one day.

Factors being discussed in experiential marketing

Bad sound

Why is the ambient sound at Carluccio's so overwhelming? Research shows it's close to jumbo-jet-landing-loud. Why? Brilliant otherwise . . . sorry, what did you say?

Good sound

And did you know Julian Treasure, a world-famous accoustician and founder of The Sound Agency who deal in 'BrandSound' and branded sound, has done work which apparently shows convincingly that playing the sound of birdsong in BAA outlets increases sales there by 10 per cent. Tweet, tweet!

Smell

Did you know that ScentAir by spraying a constant scent of baby powder in baby departments in department stores shows sales go up as a result? And that ScentAir have gone into partnership with Muzak?

Total mobile brand experience

In Australia they are big on creating experiential settings. Thus Southern Comfort has created quick assembly mobile night clubs. Castlemaine XXXX has created something called Truckmania and the Gold Retreat, a big two-storey bar which is assembled quickly providing a bar, terrace and stage on which brand lovelies create a dance floor so everyone can party – and they do party, drinking lots of beer in the meantime. It launched in 2008 and looks a fun experience.

🔘 brilliant examples

The retail theatre

- The Apple store in Regent Street is a brilliant example of how confident a brand Apple is (and how popular).

- The same with Niketown.

- Prada in New York is a ravishing experience of effortless superiority and rich minimalism. Its vast sweep of wooden boards descending into an undulation of mannequins and then rising again has to be seen to be understood. And do you feel different about Prada after going in there? You bet you do. Sharon Richey of Because Experiential Marketing tells us how it works:

'Its job is to filter all the sensory stimuli coming in and decide what we should focus our attention on at any particular moment. It's at the heart of why experiential marketing is such an effective medium.'

- St Pancras. A pantheon of Europhilia and Victorian splendour brought to twenty-first-century life. It's an amazing and rich experience. Giles Coren – francophobe – wants to take visiting French around triumphantly saying, 'See!! See!!'

- Millennium Bridge. Opens up St Paul's to new eyes. Even that swaying when it first opened was an experience.

Adding a new dimension to presentation

Experiential marketing is about leveraging the sensual aspects of a brand. When you do it well and memorably it's brilliant. Quite often, unless you are skilled and careful, it's a waste of money.

> brilliant experiential marketing is potentially very, very sexy

Brilliant experiential marketing is seductive and fun and potentially very, very sexy. Using all the senses:

● Touch

● Sight

● Smell

● Sound

● Taste

And three others:

● Dreams

● Love

● Nostalgia

brilliant tip

The next time you are in involved in an exhibition or an in-store event see if you can manage to get an expert to dream up an arsenal of sensual experiences. Creating something exciting using film, dispensed scent, sounds, taste and touch may surprise everyone and sell a lot of goods.

Experiential developments create stand-out

The need to stand out in a retail environment sometimes makes one wish one had more weapons. But honestly they do now exist. Weapons to astound you (technology has come on so far that with a virtual reality helmet on you could be anywhere).

The real insight is that we all want experience at first hand, which is the reason the best theme parks have done so well and why so much investment is going into revving up the buzz. But it's not just theme parks. As sales of CDs fade so the demand for live performance soars. When Prince gave his last CD release away free he was doing so as a flier for his hugely successful live performances at the O2 stadium. Tina Turner tickets there go for £125 – about the same as good seats at Glyndebourne or Covent Garden.

So today live experience is the thing. Customers expect it.

CHAPTER 14

Buzz marketing – when everyone starts talking about you

How 'buzz marketing' works

What it stands for today is more important than anything else. Buzz marketing is the stuff that people set up which gets word of mouth going. Something which turns enough heads in enough places and which gets a brand on the mental map. It will usually take the form of an event, a happening (an unplanned event), a stunt, street theatre, an idea which grabs people's attention and gets free media or something a little out of the ordinary. This is definitely not textbook stuff.

> buzz marketing is the stuff that gets a brand on the mental map

brilliant tip

Remember who's in charge because it's no longer us – the marketers.

'For the first time the consumer is boss, which is fascinatingly frightening, scary and terrifying because everything we used to do, everything we used to know, will no longer work.'

Kevin Roberts – Saatchi & Saatchi.

The implications of customer power

We shall have to work with the consumer more closely and with greater skill. This is going to be more like marriage than marketing. Now we have to look for more interactivity and sharing brand ownership with them. As the Coca-Cola fiasco with New Coke in 1985 showed – consumers and customers are in charge. Coca-Cola also discovered the brand is stronger in consumer than bottler hands.

And if we don't get satisfaction we can always go and moan eloquently on the web or do what I heard someone did recently, which was go and sit in the reception of a large corporation saying loudly but politely, 'I am a customer and I demand to see the CEO at once.'

What has changed

This category didn't exist when I first entered marketing except in the generalised form of 'promotional activity' or stuff that was described as being 'below the line'. For the purposes of simplicity I'm going to enclose 'buzz', 'ambient', 'guerilla', 'high impact' and 'stunt' marketing under this broad category, which signs up as a cousin of PR and event marketing. It sits in a category of cheap creativity because few of the activities are mind-wateringly expensive. However, what it represents and ultimately stands for is the kind of bravery of attitude that Nike demonstrated early on in its existence.

This is where the true spirit of marketing lies – in not having enough money and therefore having to think creatively.

we have no money so
we shall have to think

As Lord Rutherford, the physicist, once said, 'We have no money so we shall have to think.'

How to make a bit of a splash

Carlsberg mounted a 'we don't do litter' campaign in 2007, which comprised spending £5000 by dropping £20 and £50 notes randomly on to London streets each bearing a sticker on which the campaign message appeared. Great buzz. (I have Lucy Pearce at Wax Live to thank for this one.)

Brilliant marketing is all about creating a noise, getting attention, then surfing the wave of public interest and getting a smile.

Word of mouth is not an accident – you have to work at it, just as you have to work at fame. Madonna didn't get to be an icon by singing nicely – take a look at what she did – from taking her knickers off and hanging over a wall in that great arty book, *Sex*, to dressing in odd ways, to singing surprising music. She is always just ahead of the audience, keeping them guessing. And being magnificently fit – she and Mick Jagger should be examples to us all in looking good and always seemingly being in charge of the news agenda and in creating loads of buzz. Creating buzz is achieved quite often by doing the really smart thing.

NOT THIS.

But this.

Whispering loudly.

Sometimes you can get more attention by speaking softly and clearly.

Buzz is about three things

i)   **being relevant** – you can't cut into consciousness if you aren't on the consumers' radar screen. You'll just be noise.

ii)   **being accessible** – if you aren't their kind of person then however good the message you have you'll struggle. Example: M&S tying to reach most teenage kids = disconnect.

iii) **being different** – we seek innovation the whole time. Being ordinary is 'soooo boring' ... zzzzzzzzzzzzzzzzz ... 'Same as ... same as' is a description of 'yawn'. So unless you do whatever your buzz idea is with a bit of originality you will sink, not quite so much without trace, but expensively and to snorts of derision.

How to focus on key people to maximise the buzz

Focus on 'opinion formers', people who can enlarge and embellish your story. Identify the people in a group who can carry, embellish and dramatise the message, those whom Malcolm Gladwell, best-selling author of *The Tipping Point, Blink* and *The Outliers,* calls 'mavens'. Understand what will make them 'laugh' and create a buzz by saying those key words on every web site ... 'check out xxx' ... Invite them, along with as many others as you can, into your club ... give them ample, generous samples ... share with them ... indulge them. Let them enjoy your experience. Get them to say how good it was. Merchandise testimonials.

Have the courage to run chat-rooms where your customers can criticise you. That's what Apple does. They solicit complaints, admit errors and put things right. Remember that the truth is your strongest weapon. And spread the word. Always use 'tell a friend' instructions – buzz is a constant interesting and interested-sounding noise. Never stop making it.

Be exciting and don't be a control freak

You will never get word of mouth going by being ordinary or by spreading propaganda or an ordinary advertising strapline. Some, like Nike's, aren't ordinary. You have to take a few risks and once the buzz is going you have lost control anyway and the consumer will take over.

Buzz marketing is like skating on black ice. A bit dangerous but awesome if you pull it off.

Some of the most interesting 'buzz work' has been done by 'flash mobs' – strangers co-ordinated by text to appear at a given public place and act out some performance then leave.

IE (Improv Everywhere) appear in New York and have now acquired some fame for, for instance, repeating a five-minute sequence of events in a Starbucks coffee shop over and over again for an hour. Or flooding a Best Buy store with members dressed exactly like the staff. Or appearing on the subway without trousers for the now regular event 'no pants day'. When asked why they aren't wearing any, respondents simply say, 'I forgot them.'

How strategic can you be?

Here's where the Nike School of marketing (if it isn't damaging and if you like it and you think the consumer will like it, just do it) runs head on into the marketing attitude of a Kodak who will do nothing if there's a strategic disconnect. In the end you have to value how positive the buzz will be in relation to the time and effort involved.

Ultimately, the return on your investment really does matter.

 **brilliant** examples

● **Queues, spontaneous events and happenings**. This is what Ben & Jerry's did brilliantly, as did Snapple, creating parties or events on the web or by text inviting people to sample their products at a given place ▶

at a given time. Someone who worked with them advised that one of the keys was to be very, very generous in sampling. So they created events – seemingly spontaneous happenings* – and then serviced them brilliantly. If you want to create a great party to get everyone to let their hair down – and give them good reason to attend – create an imaginative invitation. If they don't end up loving your product a bit more why would you bother doing this? But if they do, you may have some more committed customers. Like extemporised theatre, no one is really unprepared but is smart enough to let the whole thing adopt its own momentum a bit like a really good party.

● **This is a story of 'Ambush Marketing' in which Nike** usurped the main sponsor, Adidas, at the Atlanta Olympics in 1996 by simply buying up all the trackside posters and poster sites in the city for the period of the Olympics. Unsurprisingly this was a one-off. At the 2008 Beijing Olympics, for instance, all the poster sites were held by the governing body who then sold them on to sponsors.

● **Agent Provocateur**. Sexy lingerie. And a bit naughty. Quite a bit naughtier than anything else in the high street. But I think it was that wonderful line which hit the street 'More S&M than M&S' that did the business for them. Great PR and, like Avis with Hertz, always clever to compare a small brand with a huge brand.

● **Sony Ericsson** had a smart idea with a new improved mobile phone with a great camera. Actors employed by the company got tourists to take photos of them with this brand new object and then explained the product when the tourists asked questions. Sort of 'reverse-chugging'. Word got out that something new and interesting was about. People started talking.

● **Cranks** was a vegetarian restaurant chain. Guinness, its owner, wanted to sell it. They wanted to create a buzz around the chain which was ailing in a soft-selling, rope-sandalled sort of way, prior to putting it on the market. The buzzy idea was to 'cast' the cutest, sweetest calf you've ever seen and walk it around the concourse of Charing Cross Station

*a 'happening' is contrived to seem spontaneous, but is usually carefully planned.

wearing a placard – a sort of sandwich-cow if you see what I mean – which said 'Make my day, eat at Cranks'. The two most powerful human reactions are 'Aaarrggg!!!' and 'Ahhh!!!!' This was definitely an 'Ahh!' moment.

- **Drive-U-home**. No one's got lavatory advertising right yet, but the guys doing a 'we'll drive you home in your own car if you're pissed in this pub' in pub urinals, just when you are reflecting that driving is a really bad idea, should hopefully have done well. Brilliant target marketing.

- **Cool**. Want to say your new car is really cool? The stunt pulled by DDB (the advertising agency) for VW in 2004 was to sculpt the car in ice full size and place it parked in a London street. It took 12 hours to melt.

- **Danger–ous!!** Stunts create buzz because danger and record-breaking turns us all on. Eating more mince pies in a minute than anyone else is at least a story and stories are the fuel of buzz. Unipart. Geniuses of logistics. A rare story of balance ... which is what logistics is all about. The world's highest tightrope walk between two hot air balloons at some 10,000 feet. Ian Ashpole, the best risk manager I've ever met, Chief Pilot of Flying Pictures, did it to massive media coverage. Buzz. And fun. And just a bit dangerous.

brilliant tip

If you are relatively new to marketing then here is a wonderful place to find out how a buzz is created. If you are a bit more senior, this is a great opportunity to work with newer members of your team and renew your own enthusiasm for 'off the wall' ideas. Your chance to see what would happen if your brand let its hair down a bit.

Brilliant word of mouth: gather round and listen

- **Where**: The places where buzz occurs will not be in conventional media.

- **How**: The whole idea of buzz is to ambush the consumer with an idea they find funny or like (in his own way, the best example of buzz in advertising was that funny orange Tango man who went around smacking people).

- **Who**: The key in 'buzz' is to target tightly – best of all opinion-formers who'll pass it on.

- **Who's in charge**: If you find this interesting remember you can't guarantee being in control of it. You are setting something up which may be taken over by the consumer. Look at Facebook parties.

- **Checklist**: Is the core idea broadly brand relevant; easily accessible to the consumer; different? (If it's been done before forget it.)

- **What**: Remember this is the world of rumour and craze. It's the world of jokes. A good joke gets everywhere in hours now. Does your buzz idea have those sort of legs? Buzz is for younger rather than older markets. Buzz and alcohol go well together.

Most of all 'buzz' is fun and pantomime. Serious brands that take themselves seriously hate it. Buzz is for the rebellious and those who want to make £1 look like £10.

Brilliant buzz is when brilliant marketing really breaks free.

CHAPTER 15

Digital marketing – nothing will be the same again

What digital marketing is

Digital marketing is anything to do with the web or mobile phones (they are increasingly important). It allows marketers to reach people on the move; to interact with people. Your phone knows where you are through GPS. So it can suggest the best Indian restaurants within half a mile. Digital involves everything from the creation of the web sites, the marketing of web sites through search engines, the use of chatrooms and communities like Facebook and LinkedIn. Digital is the prime weapon of choice for anyone under 30.

> digital is the prime weapon of choice for anyone under 30

brilliant tip

Because the sector is moving so fast and has so many different opportunities it's really smart to spend some time with someone who knows what's going on and whom you can understand.

Keeping up with the pace

a. web sites have become commodised. Learn the ways a dramatic web site like Gleneagles varies from a standard site for say a middle-of-the-road brand. Ask yourself how you use web sites and how they work or don't work.

b. We live in an open society. Knowledge used to be power. Now sharing is power. Unless you understand the concept of sharing and catalysts you won't understand digital marketing. Read *The Starfish and the Spider: The Unstoppable Power of Leaderless Organizations*, by Ori Brafman and Rod A. Beckstrom.

What's changed and is changing?

Everything, but it could have changed faster.

Just imagine ... if Bernbach, Abbott, Hegarty, Bullmore, Saatchi, Trott or others had had this medium fully available in their time, then the power of digital would have long been beyond question. Because they were all of them geniuses in the business of persuasion and inspiration.

These numbers tell a story, but only part of the story:

Fact: Advertising spend on the web exceeded advertising spend on TV in the UK last year.

Fact: 60 per cent of marketers are looking to increase their natural and paid-for-search budgets in the next 12 months – more than any other aspect of digital marketing.

Fact: Digital is a future ... but if it's *the* future we'd better be sure we are in brilliant control. The alternative is to have a transport system of skateboarders or surfers. Cool, young, but only part of the solution to getting about efficiently.

Purple cows and speed dating

Seth Godin of *Purple Cow* fame (well you would take notice of a purple cow in a field wouldn't you?) has this to say about the web:

'The internet is going to change marketing before it changes anything else . . . and increasingly there are only two kinds of company – brave and dead.'

In his book, *Permission Marketing*, he argues that we are facing a shortage of attention and money to spend on the vast array of marketing options and media that is available. 'Interruption marketing' he calls it (that is what we used to do) is a hugely expensive form of normal mass marketing and is self-negating. The more you do, the more you have to do just to keep up. Interrupting people and getting applauded is tough. Just try it in ordinary conversation and you'll find it's not how to win friends. He engagingly describes it as being like walking into a singles bar and approaching every girl one after another and asking them to marry you until one says 'yes'. In contrast, permission marketing is just like dating. If all goes well you go on another date. And one thing may lead to another.

Permission marketing turns strangers into friends into lifetime customers. Many of the rules of dating apply, as do many of the benefits.

The medium where you can achieve this is likely to be the web.

Fact: No sane marketer or business won't have a web site and won't spend increasing money and time worrying about it.

Fact: Networking has become institutionalised with Facebook, LinkedIn and so on. But there are over 40 major sites now and these are the top six in terms of traffic:

1 MySpace 245m – general site – big in USA, Canada, Europe.

2 Facebook 124m – general – 600 per cent growth in the last 12 months.

3 Windows Live Spaces 120m – blogging – previously MSN Spaces.

4 Habbo 100m – chatroom – 31 worldwide communities.

5 hi5 75m – general, Cyprus, Latin America, Portugal, Romania.

6 Orkut 67m – Google, Brazil, Paraguay, India. Not liked in USA.

Confused? You should be. MySpace has the population of the USA pretty well. Eat your heart out NBC. And Facebook describes itself as a 'social utility that connects you with people around you'.

Fact: spam is the biggest communication phenomenon in the world today. So what was in my junk file over the past two days? Only 360 messages. Subjects? Sex aids about 35 per cent, including one claiming it would turn my bedroom life into a volcano of pleasure; watches about 10 per cent; other luxury branded goods 10 per cent; gambling 15 per cent; over-the-counter degrees and PhDs 5 per cent; cheap credit 5 per cent; Tesco and other supermarket vouchers 5 per cent; travel offers/foreign homes 5 per cent; others 10 per cent – a motley bunch including 'Explore Kent', Autoglass Repair, Beefeater Free Meal Offer and free music downloads. All over the place and a waste of my time . . . the unacceptable face of digital marketing.

Fact: The usage of email is changing. The 18–35-year-old demographic use of email is falling quite quickly. Fed up with the volumes of spam and provided with alternatives such as chatrooms, instant messaging and social networking, they use email about half as much in their social and personal life as an older demographic will. Even at work, where they are obliged to use it

the role of email as a marketing tool is changing

because it is the de facto communications system, they seek alternatives when they can (including the telephone).

The jury is out on whether this is a change of behaviour, or an age-related thing that will not carry across into future behaviour, but once established, habits are hard to break. So the role of email as a marketing tool is changing.

Questions you must ask and things you should do

- Does your email support your brand claims using truth not hyperbole, and admitting errors ... lie on the web and die on the web.

- You'll need much tighter segmentation of your lists of users than usual to recognise and reward advocates and complainants.

- You'll need to mine other routes, like the customer service, and have a strong engagement with social network sites.

- The average number of 'friends' in the 18–25-year-old demographic in the US in social networking is 102. So if an email recipient adds something from your email (or the email itself) to their Facebook page, all these friends are emailed an alert automatically: 'Richard has added this content', etc. So this gives a multiplier of two orders of magnitude – plus a personal intro/endorsement from the Facebook person.

If spam is the unacceptable face then the acceptable face lies in great Google ideas like Google Earth, which enables you to see the earth from space down to street-level detail; Google Alert, which searches specific topics for you on a daily or weekly basis – your own researcher; and Google Zeitgeist, which tells you what's going on and where it's at in different countries.

brilliant examples

Other digital marketing ideas and developments

- **Lenovo** at the Olympics – they called it 'Lenovo Voices of the Olympics' and recruited 100 bloggers from 25 counties to talk about 27 sports – 1500 blog posts were created, which generated over 8000 comments in a month, and there was widespread mention on social web sites with over 10 million social media impressions; 16m new visitors went to the Lenovo web site during the games. Activity was integrated effectively with the cherry on the cake being the masses of Lenovo machines in the iLounges for the media and athletes – creating over 30,000 active users. The idea of making Lenovo an Olympic language was smart, as was recruiting a passionate sales force on the web.

- **Ben & Jerry's web site**. I love this site about how the cows are massaged. Full of quirk and fun like this:

  'They (Ben and Jerry) soon became popular in the local community for the finest all natural ice cream. Ben had no sense of taste so he relied on what he called 'mouth feel', so big chunks of chocolate, fruit and nut became their signature. While they disagreed at times over the chunk size, they did agree that they wanted to enjoy themselves – as Jerry put its "If it's not fun, why do it?"'

- **The Bud Light 'Swear Jar'** on YouTube. When good, old-fashioned advertising meets bright, new shiny online. Brilliant ******* stuff. By the way, do beware what you put on Facebook or YouTube. All executive search companies trawl these sites to check out on any unsuitable behaviour from potential candidates.

- **The McDonald's web site**. After years of grotty PR, two CEOs dying of cancer in quick succession and in 2004 Morgan Spurlock's film *Supersize Me*, the giant looked as if it were on its knees. It tried to market salads but is now back to its core tasty values with a web site that addresses issues – try www.makeupyourownmind.co.uk where questions like 'what's in our burgers?' are charmingly answered: 'There's nothing sinister. It's just beef.' They serve 2.5 million customers a day and sales are still growing. They have kept the faith with their founder Ray Kroc's, edict: 'Look after the customer and the business will look after itself.' This web site is rich in good stuff and is brilliantly confident.

- **New ideas on symposia**. I'm told that there are organisations that allow people in specific interest groups out there to vote for the agendas of a symposium, get experts to address these items, open them up for debate, create what they'd call a record or an archive of thought leadership and publish it online – sort of Wikipedia on the run … fascinating times we live in. Brilliant opportunities.

- **The Doctors.net.uk story**. The company was launched in 1998, the web was barely off the ground, the need was to build a critical mass of doctors so the networking effect of a working community would create its own momentum. Without a large, active membership, they couldn't expect revenues … so losses piled up – shades of Amazon. In order to maximise a limited budget, and give credibility to a new source of information, education and collaboration for the medical profession, they built partnerships with powerful existing medical institutions as they needed their credibility within the profession. These, in turn, were old institutions, struggling to establish a presence in the new world of the internet. Joint marketing initiatives were set up with the General Medical Council; the result of a collaborative marketing approach with the Medical Protection Society, the Medical Defence Union and the Medical Sickness Society was membership growth that far exceeded plan, and today www.Doctors.net.uk has virtually every doctor in the UK as a member. The early collaborative activities with major medical institutions not only gave fast membership growth, but qualified www.Doctors.net.uk as *the* professional medical web site of choice. It's such a great concept. The medical intranet. By giving access to all the latest medical and pharmaceutical developments this is a brilliant way of sharing best practice and saving time. But pity the poor, redundant pharmaceutical salesman; and check out the web site: http://www.doctors.net.uk/about/home.htm

The convergence of mobile phones and computers raises issues about cinematically complex web sites having to work on mobile platforms. And increasingly the web is going to be the medium on which you watch films and use for your free Skype telephone calls.

Summary

i) **Alliances are what this is about**. Work with marketing minds who understand the commercial possibilities, not just the technology which is, frankly, boring. Such people do exist. Anything is possible nowadays – you'd better believe it.

ii) **Think forward into change**. Think about how your own life is changing and consider how a combination of web site, text, blogs, social networks, e-newsletters and viral advertising might combine to create a real momentum in marketing a brand.

search engine marketing ... where the smart money is

iii) **SOS for SEM**. Get the very best help you can on search engine marketing – the way of driving people to your site. It's where the smart money is.

iv) **Have fun**. Don't be bemused by the technology, but reflect on the joy of pretty well instantaneous changes to copy. Think about customising your messages. Find a conversational as opposed to a corporate tone of voice.

v) **Geek or genius**? But do not confuse technical brilliance with marketing brilliance. Being Lenovo at the Olympics sounds brilliant, but we shall see if the idea was big enough to really stick in the mind.

The best ideas and the cleverest thinking will always beat the smartest metadata.

Conclusion

Here's what Steve Ballmer, the head of Microsoft, says about what's going on and, let's face it, he should know. Steve is, for once, quite reflective:

'The future of the way people consume information, the way they socialise and connect is going to change a lot more in the next ten years than in the last ten.'

The driver of this activity is going to be the consumer rather than the marketer, so here's the most brilliant advice I can give you.

Keep your eyes peeled, keep your ear to the ground, keep your nose to the grindstone and avoid clichés.

This is a revolution of the people, not just of marketers, and it feels good.

CHAPTER 16

Branded entertainment – when programmes and advertising join together (and other wacky ideas)

How branded entertainment works

Branded entertainment is sponsored TV or film. Soap operas were originally called that because they were sponsored by Procter and Gamble, makers of – soap. This world is being reinvented with power and focus. Sir Martin Sorrell for one, and his is the loudest voice in marketing services, believes that sponsoring films and TV series is going to be the next big thing.

What has changed?

A few years ago product placement was much in the news. It began to get particularly bad press as it seemed to be overdone in James Bond films and *Coronation Street*. They'd stand in that ghastly shop in front of bars of Wispa, packs of Typhoo or bottles of Irn Bru or whatever, and the camera focused on the products

branded entertainment may be the future of broadcast marketing

with indecent morbidity. And Ofcom seemed to turn a blind eye. But this branded entertainment concept is something different and a whole lot more exciting. It may indeed be the future of broadcast marketing. Think of your 'brand' as the 'executive producer'. Think of the next local pantomime as being written with a brand in mind. Imagine Cinderella being sponsored by a shoe brand. Timberland brings you Cinderella in the 'shoe that fits' – you get the idea.

It's all happening

All the big names are getting in on this phenomenon with Coca-Cola launching a TV series called 'Stepping Stones' on NBC in the summer of 2009; P&G launching a new flavoured toothpaste on the American version of *The Apprentice*; and Amex, Budweiser, Toyota and Ford – they're all at it. In the UK we have the Nokia Green Room on Channel 4.

And it's not just about TV

Fay Weldon wrote *The Bulgari Connection*. *Somers Town*, the well-reviewed, award-winning film that Eurostar pumped £500,000 into and *Pot Noodle: The Musical*, which actually stars someone from the commercial, hit the Edinburgh Fringe in 2008. When something hits the Fringe, as a marketing man I start to be interested because at the back of my mind I hear the word 'CASH'.

New ways of engaging consumers

Here's what Nick Chapman, brand strategy director at Venables, Bell and Partners in San Francisco, says:

'Advertisers are realising that if they create their own content they don't need to pay for ad space, they have greater control over how

their brand is portrayed and ideally they create a more in-depth and involving interaction between consumer and brand.'

Good stuff, Nick. But wait. Here comes his caveat.

'Brands tend to want to be shiny and positive while people generally prefer entertainment about complicated people doing stupid or dirty things to each other.'

Nick Chapman is spot on and he's right to be so uncorporate. The way in which real people speak is going to be the language of the future; much as the Simpsons talk about ABC and Fox (their broadcaster) – full of mock-contempt, but with confidence and affection too.

> the way in which real people speak is going to be the languge of the future

Shiny and positive belongs to the era of 'big, bland and boring'. Today's work needs to be authentic and edgy.

This is new and exciting territory

In the future, advertising agencies are going to work with producers on content, making brands the new patrons of great movies and shows. It's going to mean the money to do great work will be available. It may spell the resuscitation of commercial TV.

In the brilliant world of marketing we are going to create 'brand architects' who will spend their time working out precisely what their brand is and what their brand is not and how the perfect fit with a film, series, play or TV event can be constructed. And unlike in the past, the associations are going to be subtle and interwoven not crude. The issues are going to be understanding exactly what emotional territory you want to occupy and how available it can be made.

What this means to an average marketer

Probably not a lot at the moment ... except as an intelligent marketer they should be speculating what it could mean. But watch this space and consider how you might create something like *Pot Noodle: The Musical*. With so many arts festivals being started up, the opportunity may be closer than you think. *Guinness: The Epic*; *Samsung: The Opera* and so on.

What is clear is the need to be smart enough to think how you could exploit a property without spoiling it. If you could, how would you change your favourite TV programme so it could work in partnership with a brand – what would change? For example, the news. You'd probably want to have a new take on the ITV 'And Finally' slot called, let us suppose, 'The Good News Now From Brand X'.

The opportunities for major brands and major programmes and niche brands and niche programmes seem immense, especially if the old order breaks down. What happens, for instance, if the BBC loses its licence in the future? A lot of hot properties may be looking for patrons.

Summary

- **Marketing exploitation is in play**. In the current world the rules on product placement seem likely to relax.
- **Controlling content takes us somewhere new**. More excitingly it seems that branded entertainment may become a new form of sponsorship, but with brands having some authorial influence on content.
- **Having fun for everyone**. Here (as Pot Noodles has shown) is a way of giving the brand and its consumer the opportunity to have a bit of fun.
- **Understand what the consumer will take**. Provided the aim is to make what is done agreeable, sensitive and

welcome to the consumer, this may be a huge opportunity for marketing breakthrough.

- **Big brands need big ideas. All brands need affordable ideas**. Any brilliant marketer is going to track what the big brands are doing here and seeing what works. I can't wait to see the Orvis Fishing programme or the Callaway Golf series.

- **When brand patrons create best-sellers it's time to watch out**. The acid test will be when a big brand helps create a top rating favourite series. Then we'll see the world turn on its head. Then we'll see Hollywood and Wall Street get very, very friendly with each other.

- **The news of the future** . . . When a Heinz gets credited with inventing the next Simpsons the world will have moved on.

Afterthoughts and possibilities

- **This is the big news** . . . but what is happening goes beyond 'buzz marketing'. New media and marketing opportunities are being created the whole time.

- **Paint the town pink**. They did it for Barbie.

- **Sponsor local communities**. Imagine Basildon – political bellweather of the UK – having funds poured into it by the *Sun*.

- **Theatre in the cinema**. They did it with a film being stopped – the manager (an actor) climbing on to the stage and asking if 'a Mrs Whatever' is in the audience – she is (an actress) and drama ensues – a fatal car crash . . . Go on – you choose the plot. Very disturbing.

- **Brand pigeons**. A genius painted brand names on the breasts of pigeons in Times Square. Not popular with animal lovers.

- **The Heathrow Express is/was RBS**. What a great way of reaching and reassuring the business community.

PART 3

Creating and executing a great marketing plan

The nitty-gritty part of the story

CHAPTER 17

The first steps in creating a marketing campaign

Decide how you want to play this

Not all forms of marketing are the same. If you are working as a brand manager at Procter and Gamble, or if you are organising a fund-raising concert in your local community, the rules are somewhat different even though the principles are similar. So to start with, be very clear which of these three situations you are in:

i)   DIY marketing where you have very little budget available and where what you are involved in is probably a 'one off'.

ii) You are in a small business (maybe even your own business) and every penny is going to count. You are still going to behave totally professionally, but you aren't thinking about million-pound campaigns. This will influence all your thinking.

iii) You are in the marketing department of a big and serious marketing company with access to a lot of professional resources internally and externally. You should still have an 'every penny has to count' attitude, but your options are somewhat more extensive.

Where do you start?

By asking yourself a few very simple questions.

- What are you trying to achieve?
- How much do you have to achieve it with?
- Over what period of time do you have to achieve this?

And by recognising that you will have to consider and position yourself so you have the equipment to make a decision on the following:

- A brief that any supplier would find helpful and which helps you clearly organise your thoughts.
- The core message that you want to communicate.
- A plan of activity that is broadly costed, incorporating the kind of activity and the key ingredients – think of this as your battle plan.
- How you are going to buy all the components and your strategy for this, so anyone asking 'did you think of using . . . ?' can be given a considered answer rather than being met with a blank stare.
- What resources and team do you have available?
- Remember, however, that this is an iterative process. You are sketching a plan not laying concrete foundations. The process is one where a sudden blinding insight can transform everything. But you have to start somewhere and this is the professional way of proceeding.

Writing a brief

Now write a very simple brief; and briefs are not called brief for nothing so keep it short and to the point. The discipline of writing a brief will focus your mind whether you are at P&G or a local book club. Also, there are two sorts of brief – the one off or launch brief and the brief you'd write for an ongoing campaign for an existing brand.

A brief brief

1 **The product or service** – what is it, what does it do, who is it for, where do I get it, why is it good, who is the owner/promoter of it and what, in a nutshell, are they all about?

2 **The competition** – who and what are they, how do they compare in price, quality, presentation, people, star-appeal, benefits and size?

3 **What does this campaign have to do?** – e.g. sell something, open the door for someone to sell something, merely inform, change a given group's opinion about something and so on. Avoid the temptation of asking for more than one thing to be done. And if you can't do that, isolate the most important task.

4 **What is the key message?** – e.g. the book *Brilliant Marketing* gives you the knowledge and equipment to be a great marketer.

5 **Are there any specific challenges to overcome?** – these might be the economy, recent competitive activity, adverse news coverage, suspicions that your product is inferior to others, anything – this is 'be honest time'.

6 **What will success look like?** – try and put a number on this – don't be vague.

7 **What's your budget?**

8 **What other resources do you have?** – people, free material, premises, anything you can think of?

A longer brief

This is a longer version only because it is about a brand, product or service at a moment in time so there's history to take into account as well as the likelihood of the competitive landscape being more intense.

1 **The product or service** – what is it, what does it do, who is it for, who in fact uses it, how many loyal users, occasional users, lapsed users, non-users do you think or know there are, where do they get it, why is it good, who is the owner/promoter of it and what, in a nutshell, are they all about, how is it doing in sales and market share terms?

2 **The competition** – who and what are they, how do they compare in price, quality, presentation, people, star appeal, benefits and size. Who uses each competitor, what is their user profile in terms of loyal, occasional, lapsed and non-users, which competitors are on the way up or down and why, what is the share profile in the market sector?

3 **What does this campaign have to do?** – e.g. defend a position, grow sales, grow share, grow profit (perhaps by preserving sales after a price increase), open the door for someone to sell something, merely inform, change a given group's opinion about something, build a story to provide the opportunity for long-term growth and so on. Avoid the temptation of asking for more than one thing to be done, and if you can't do that isolate the most important task.

4 **What is/are the unique assets, characteristics of your product?** – also list all the characteristics that may not be unique but are interesting and worth talking about.

5 **What does the consumer think?** – is there any research – if so summarise the key findings. Specifically what are the good and not so good things. Be blunt not bland in your descriptions, and in the sector as a whole see if you can

define what it is that is most important to the potential consumer.

6 **How does the consumer feel?** – do you have any evidence or intuition about the way the consumer or potential consumer might feel emotionally towards products in the sector and towards the sector as a whole. Think of words like boring, exciting, fun, functional, prestigious, satisfying, interesting, stimulating, nostalgic, impressive and so on.

7 **What is the key message?** – e.g. the Brilliant series gives you the knowledge and equipment to be great at work in a way no other books do.

8 **Are there any specific challenges to overcome?** – these might be the economy, recent competitive activity, adverse news coverage, suspicions that your product is inferior to others, anything – this is 'be honest time'.

9 **How do you want people to feel about this campaign?** – your loyal users, your non-users – people you want to convert, your competitors, your staff and colleagues.

10 **What will success look like?** – try and put a number on this – don't be vague.

11 **What's your budget?**

12 **What other resources do you have?** – people, free material, premises, anything you can think of that might be useful.

If you simply don't have the information say so, but it wouldn't hurt to ask yourself why not, and see what it would take to get a steer in the right direction; because the more you know, the better the brief will be. And the eventual plan will be more robust and more likely to work.

Finding the right message

This is the key. If you say the right thing in the right way you are more likely to persuade your audience to do what you want.

Which is stating the obvious, but it's intriguing how often this is misunderstood. Some of the most obscure and daft bits of advertising or promotion have you scratching your head and asking yourself why they didn't say the obvious thing like Carlsberg did when they said 'possibly the best lager in the world' – confident and strong.

brilliant tip

Sit down with as many people as possible who stimulate or inspire you to talk about your brief, your mission and where you have got so far. This is very much a case of many heads being better than one at this early formative stage.

Things to think about

macho language and a killer message are unlikely to work

Be clear who it is you most need to talk to – nowadays it's increasingly likely to be a woman, so macho language and a killer message (unless you are Nike) are unlikely to work.

Assemble all the good stuff you have to say about your product. Even though you probably won't use all this, it will help those whom you brief – PR people, direct marketers, advertising people and so on – to get a good sense of the richness of your product quality, its superiority and your confidence in it. And if you are light on budget and are doing this campaign virtually or entirely single-handed, it will help you get a great sense of your sales story. Imagine you have to present to a roomful of people and by the sheer power and depth of your story and oratory convince them to say 'yes'.

Don't be too subtle.

Focus on the 'what it is', 'why you need it' part of the message. Do not allow yourself to be accused of producing a message that has people saying, 'I didn't know what it was for.'

Always think about where the message will be seen and the nature of the challenges posed. For example – don't let anyone persuade you that an essay on a poster site is a good idea.

What a brief might look like

This was the brief to relaunch a management consultancy whose fictional name will be Turret & Partners.

CREATIVE BRIEF FOR THE RELAUNCH OF TURRET & PARTNERS

Background

Historically Turret has been more focused on process functions producing rather dull and lifeless material to describe what it does. It has determined the time is right to give itself a makeover and present itself as a key, lively, customer- (people) focused operation. An operation that is into thought leadership not just getting things done. The administrative aspect needs to improve as well but the key change is that it will do more things, better and faster. The design of literature and everything associated with Turret needs to reflect this intent.

The product/service

- What – Turret encompasses everything from HR advice to outsourcing – all the administrative housekeeping stuff which needs to be got right fast and first time. But then there's talent and

▶

leadership development at which Turret has especial skills.

- Where – throughout Europe
- Who inside – all the team within Turret
- Who outside – all existing and potential clients
- How – Turret is set upon developing the business into being a leading edge practitioner not just another consultancy.

What's changing

- To the service – the intent is to change from being a tactical resource to being a business partner function. Increasingly Turret will be a facilitator of change and a developer of business leaders. This is already broadly in place in the UK but needs to be set in place in Europe and globally if Turret is to optimise its competitive advantages.

- To the constituency – not enough yet. Employees more commonly perceive Turret as a resource called in 'when there's bad news ' rather than being a positive proactive business partner, counsellor, critical friend, whose primary aim is to help all the people perform better individually and as a team.

- Overall – Turret's recent work on talent has moved it centre stage in world business. The thing that will distinguish two competing businesses is the quality of their people selection, team coaching and people management. What Turret can do now to modern management is what the team coach is to a football team. The competitive benefits lie in getting more out of people (productivity), inspiring people (morale) and in presenting a face of the business that appeals (making recruitment of talent easier).

Our main communication objectives

1 Leading edge thinking is developing fast at Turret and becoming a catalyst to growth and change

2 Our competitive advantage is our people

3 Turret is there to improve everything it does and will work as a partner with all its clients

Our key audiences

1 Our own management

2 Clients

3 Potential clients

What we want management to think and feel

1 As a manager I have lots of people issues to think about – I need a confidential business consultant who is expert on all aspects of people stuff to be there for me.

2 I want help in building and developing people in a team that will make me look good and perform well.

3 I need coaching and helping as a manager – I need to trust HR to help me when I personally need it.

What we want employees to think and feel

1 Turret has set itself a new standard

2 A strong creative consulting function = a better place to work

▶

3   When xxx works closely with top management then things will get done properly

4   Turret is a 'safe house' that always has a sensible perspective on things

What we want potential employees to think and feel

1   The stuff that irritates me with other consultants is done brilliantly here

2   I want to work with a place like that

3   They talk about talent development in a way that sounds good

4   I trust them

You are beginning to create a plan

Your brief will have helped you get a good sense of what is most likely to be useful and effective.

> once you get blasé about marketing you lose that spirit of adventure

This is where things get really exciting and where you begin to dream of creating an integrated marketing campaign that is so seamless and successful that people speak of it in awe. Never lose that thrill. Once you get blasé about marketing you lose that spirit of adventure which characterises every great brand and every great piece of communication. Now it's time to get more specific.

A totally new way of looking at brilliance is that less is more

I loved Picasso's comment to a man who saw him next to a large lump of marble and on hearing that Picasso intended to hew a horse head from it said that looked like a jolly hard thing to do. Picasso replied:

'Not really, what I have to do is chip away the bits that don't look like horse – that's all.'

What a brilliantly fresh way of looking at a problem.

Brilliance in marketing is about chipping away, finding and being thrilled by new possibilities. So let's get chipping.

CHAPTER 18

Refining objectives, messages, mood and attitude

This is an iterative intellectual process

J ust because you have written a brief and are just about to embark on writing the marketing plan on which, in a large company, you may well be judged, do not suppose the job is done. If you want to be a high-flier you have to allow yourself a few things:

Relentless interrogation

- a breathing space in which theoretically the plan and the overall thrust can 'cook'
- the opportunity for second thoughts
- the discipline of subjecting yourself to rigorous challenging. You are probably about to spend a large amount of your own money or to ask your company to invest huge amounts on your thinking and insights. Time to apply the tests of:
  - What if?
  - Why?
  - Why so much?
  - Why so little?
  - Is this ambitious enough? Is it too ambitious?
  - What could our competitors do to blow this thinking out of the water?

- Are we sure we understand how the key consumers will react?
- How much guesswork is in here?
- What factors are changing out there in the marketplace and 'real world' that we ought to be concerned about?
- Are there any aspects of this we might be able to do better or cheaper and if so what would it take?
- If you had to write a plan B with half the budget what would it be and what would the consequences be?

brilliant tip

Don't get paranoid but the best presentations and the best briefs need to undergo the fire of fierce interrogation. So take the punishment unflinchingly, reflecting as to whether the inquisitor might have a point and that your answer may be flimsy and subjective.

The objectives

the best presentations and the best briefs need to undergo the fire of fierce interrogation

In any exam, read the question several times to make sure you completely understand it. If you work for an agency make sure you completely understand the brief you are given by a client. The reason most agencies mess up is they haven't understood what they were asked to do.

Similarly with our own marketing objectives. Things change rapidly (especially nowadays). Competitors get stronger or weaker or even disappear. A triumphalist advertising campaign might not be a smart thing to run just as one is making mass redundancies. Objectives must always be seen in context.

So every so often just sense-check that they are still right and in the right order, namely that the most important is the first one. Sounds obvious? You'd be surprised.

> objectives must always be seen in context

And if there are more than three key objectives there are too many.

The marketer who has ten key objectives is going to fail – always.

You are, however, allowed to have secondary and tertiary objectives – no more than two of each, provided there is budget to support their being achieved.

Messages

These fall into three categories:

i) **The one- or two-word equity** – the key territory of which you are trying to be brand owner. It could be refreshment, luxury, superior sounding, more choice, better tasting, lower-calorie, longer-lasting. Just make sure you have clarity here and internal alignment. Not a bad idea to see if the consumer is OK with it too.

ii) **The big simple story** – we move from two words to about 22. This is the so called 'elevator pitch'; the presentation to the low-attention-threshold CEO.

iii) **Supporting evidence and story lines** – if your brand or corporation is rich in great stories that's very good news for the people in PR, but beware of being too up front with secondary stories unless they are mainly supportive, as they will distract from the focus.

Just make sure that all the stories are fireproof, are true, are appropriate in the light of events in the market, in the world outside and are going to cause no unnecessary problems.

Moods

The very act of writing down in a few words how you want your customers to feel when your marketing campaign starts, forces you to double-check that what you have in your campaign is actually consistent with what you are trying to achieve. And remember, this is very distinctly how you want your customers to feel and what you'd like their mood to be.

Attitude

The Nike case study suggests how important corporate attitude can be. A strong positive, clear and credible set of values and attitude to what you do breathes through all the great companies – Nike, Google, Apple. Sometimes, of course, they make a mistake, but the key reason their people come to work is not just about making money and increasing shareholder value. It's about winning the marketing game. It's about being smarter than the competitor and being part of a brilliant team.

Never stop refining

Keep on sense-checking what you are doing – when times change, change what you are trying to achieve and how you want to get there. You are a performer in live theatre. As we all know, live theatre audiences are different every night. Be attuned to the differences and be smart about how to maintain or wrest competitive advantage.

 **tip**

Never stop trying to improve (usually by taking stuff out).

CHAPTER 19

How to write a brilliant marketing plan

What is a marketing plan?

marketing plan is a success plan for the marketing of whatever brand, product, service or company that is the subject of the exercise. The word success is important here, as all too often I've seen take-it-or-leave-it exercises which leaves it for a board or investors to decide what to do next. Make no mistake that this is a *selling* document which, in almost every case, even if it's your own plan and your own cash, is asking for a large sum of

> this is a *selling* document which is asking for a large sum of money

money and justifying the investment requested. Actually it's not a request, it ought to be a foolproof case which is hard to resist.

 brilliant definition

No one bothered to explain these when I went into marketing so let me try and be more helpful to you.

A strategy is a definition of where specifically you are trying to get and what specifically you want to achieve. Just increasing profit is not much of a strategy by itself. It is only a dream, unless it's underpinned by an irrefutable strategic plan. Having said that, the most common basic strategies are share growth, sales growth, profit

▶

growth, cash growth, survival, profitable retrenchment, merger or acquisition and priming for sale

A strategic plan is a route map of how to get there (wherever it is you want to get). This will normally come with specific milestones showing where you want to be by when. A strategy and strategic plan should always go together.

A tactical plan is about the modes of transport, accommodation, diversions and the changes of plan that external factors may determine. In other words, it says in detail here what happens to whom and when and why and what the impact is anticipated to be. It is the 'getting it done manual'.

Tactics are what happens every day as you respond to the moving ball game of life. But if you divorce tactics from strategy it is, as Alice in Wonderland said, like this: 'If you don't know where you are going it doesn't much matter which road you take.' It's very confusing for everyone if you don't have a strategy.

Explaining all these issues is core to getting a team onside and understanding what they need to do.

Two others: **customer** and **consumer**. Having spent a lot of my life in fast-moving consumer goods I have a 'consumer' mentality which is all to do with frequent purchases. This excludes a lot of marketing situations like those in financial services or capital goods.

As of today – here and now in *Brilliant Marketing* – I am setting a new rule. I shall only hereafter refer to the customer be they trade customer or end user. The customer is who buys your product, brand or service. OK?

What is needed and where do you get it?

There are loads of templates available. Look on the web. Business Links is always sound, www.BusinessLink.gov.uk, as is www.businessballs.com on the SOSTAC® model.

But sound is not enough, so I'll give you my own all singing and dancing version of the BM (brilliant marketing) template in a few minutes.

It is long. It is demanding. It is focused. And it asks a lot of searching questions. Not everyone will be able to answer every question. But they have to try. The key issue is that in reading this template of a brilliant marketing plan you begin to sense just how important marketing really is. This is a very professional business.

brilliant tip

Professional marketers must have answers to all the questions that can be asked about a brand they control. If they aren't experts they aren't in control.

The brilliant marketing plan

1 **An executive summary** – no more than one page – written in English – avoid jargon. And each section in the plan needs its own one-page executive summary because this is a long document and busy executives need lots of 'memory pit-props'.

2 **The corporate background** and strategic objectives on the business overall. What is the company's mission statement? Where does this brand, service, business fit within the whole, how important is it in sales, profit and reputation? What is driving the company right now; is it possible the brand might be sold in the near future? This would be critical to the way it is developed.

▶

3   **What the brand (product or service) is** in some detail in terms of specification, pricing, packaging, variants – any information that allows an inquisitive CFO to be satisfied and impressed without having to ask you. Brand highlights (things that anyone needs to bear in mind when considering its future). A SWOT analysis should also be included, so you really interrogate the status of the brand – upsides and downsides. Some of this may be contained in an appendix to avoid overloading the main body of the plan with too much detail.

4   **Who have been the key targets?** In terms of types and classifications, gender, age, geography and so on, of customers. And precisely the same as regards the trade distribution. This is about the brand's history and its current status, it is not yet about the future.

5   **Where has the brand come from?** An overview of the history of the brand, its high points, its low points, key milestones, sales history, P&L history, investment history. Identify the key events in the past and analyse what lessons have been learned. Some of the detail here may be usefully included in an appendix.

6   **Analysis of the current situation of the brand**. Sales performance, market share performance, business performance (P&L), research highlights, changes, levels of investment planned in R&D. Current marketing spend and ROI (return on investment) plus an analysis of success and failure. The key question is this – how different is this proposed plan to the existing plan? On reading this section the true position and value of the brand should be entirely understood by any reader.

7   **Comparative analysis versus all existing competitors** (and companies potentially likely to enter the market.) This is

usually best done in tabular form with cryptic commentary and a simple crude five-point scoring system whereby a reader can easily pick up relative strengths and weaknesses. Areas that need to be covered are:

i) *Product issues.* Product design/components (in food we'd call this the recipe), how would each brand perform in a *Which* review? Innovation capability, history of innovation, quality and provenance of ingredients, any striking or unique characteristics in manufacturing process or content. Where is it manufactured? By whom and what is their reputation? What are the biggest problems each has in its formulation, design, etc. Based on their knowledge and expertise, what does the person running the brand think about the quality, value and long-term sustainability of each?

ii) *Consumer issues.* First in their minds: consumer awareness, consumer rating, if this were a stock would it be going up and down in consumer eyes and how sharply in either direction? What do consumers feel about each brand? Second, behaviour. Levels of trial, levels of repeat purchase, loyalty levels, high-commitment levels. Which brand is the biggest threat from a competitive perspective? (If each brand ceased to exist to which other brand(s) would its customers go and why?)

iii) *Distribution channel issues.* Levels of distribution: where is it strongest and weakest, what's the reputation with the trade of each brand and how is this changing and why? The same question as for consumers – when asked if the brand were a stock would they say it was going up or down and how sharply in either direction? Major recent highlights and successes. Trade strategy for each brand? Quality of trade relationships with each major

▶

account? What has happened to any recent specific
initiatives?

iv)   *Pricing*. Show all pricing on shelf and on a like-for-like
basis (viz. per gram, per unit, per hour, per whatever unit
works best). Discounting strategies and promotional
'cocktails'. What is the view of the pricing issues by
consumers and trade customers – five years ago, last year,
now and – likely – going into the future? How price
sensitive are all/any of the brands in this market? Are
there pricing variations with overseas markets?

v)   *Marketing*. Levels of investment per annum over the past
five years. Two-word equity description for each – what is
it? Marketing mix. Brand proposition from advertising – is
this different from the two-word equity. Consistency of
promotion. What is the profile/reputation in the media?
How creative is the marketing for each? What's the
biggest asset of each – how well leveraged? Biggest
weakness for each – how serious? Examples of marketing
material (all these should go in an appendix).

vi)   *Sales*. By region, by country, by outlet type, by account, by
season, historic variations. Analysis of why strengths and
weaknesses exist where they do. Compare how each sales
operation is structured. What distinguishes the sales
cultures of different competitors and different markets?

vii) *Human capital*. I find calling people 'capital' a little
offensive, but for the purposes of this and its audience I'll
live with it … So – an analysis of the respective strengths
of the highs and lows in quality and quantity of the
marketing/sales teams is relevant. Are there stars at any
company and are they really making a difference? How
stable are the competitors? Places where uncertainty is

rife (unless it is normal for the industry) may make companies vulnerable to specific attack. How and where would you do this?

viii) *Green and ethical issues*. Are there any? Ingredients, sourcing, labour force, pollution, carbon emissions, diversity of workforce, ethical and Fairtrade practices, animal welfare where relevant, health and safety issues, tribunals held or pending. Is there a clear corporate strategy available and understood about what the company stands for? Is it sustainable? Does the brand help or hinder this?

8 **The three key objectives** in the plan set against the current competitive situation the brand faces. It may seem unreasonable to force you down to three objectives, but long experience shows that if you have a very long (and no doubt worthy) list of objectives:

● Your team won't be able to get their heads round them;

● You'll forget them halfway through the year in a crisis and chances are you'll fail on all of them.

So set yourself the three things that will make the difference and put all your people, financial and emotional efforts behind delivering those.

9 **Absolute clarity on the marketing strategy** – what it and the outline strategic plan actually are. A focus on why the plan will succeed and a compelling argument as to why it is distinctive and why it is a winning plan is vital. This is such

the marketing strategy is where you take charge

an important section – this is where you take charge and literally say this is MY plan and this is why I know it will work.

10 **The current and future customer targets**. Why have they changed from previous plans? What new research evidence supports this change? Are there new ways of understanding these people and securing their long-term custom and commitment? How safe do you believe you are in retaining them? On balance are they less or more loyal and why?

11 **Compelling and detailed evidence** that there is an absolute understanding of the opportunities but, more importantly, the challenges to be overcome especially as regards

- competitive threats

- consumer attitudes

- distribution constraints and opportunities.

> do not worry about being repetitive so long as you are consistent

This is the section which in essence allows you to pick up all the good stuff in your competitive analysis (in which you are now surely a *Mastermind* champion in whatever product sector it is). Finally, you need to highlight cryptically all the key issues. Do not worry about being repetitive so long as you are consistent.

12 **Analysis of the quality and quantity of resources** needed to succeed in delivering this plan – human and financial – and the time it will take to achieve success. Do not understate (but also do not overstate) what is needed. Be entirely reasonable and forensic about this. At the same time, asking for more resources each year to achieve the same or just a little more will eventually (and rightly) lose you your job. Find in your 'Magic Marketing Mix' a way of making each marketing pound worth a little bit more each year so you get more results for less investment. It's the fastest way to promotion I know.

13 **A clear description of the milestones** that the strategic
plan has; those standards of measurement that will be used;
and the actual goals that will need to be achieved to qualify as
success. Called by many 'Action Standards' – or in English –
what we are trying to achieve (our objectives) and how close we
got to achieving or exceeding them along a series of agreed
dimensions. You define those but I'd suggest the ones that are
surely going to matter most (no doubt there are others) are
sales (or, in a downturn, retained sales and in an upturn,
conquest sales); **market share** and most of all **profit** and
ROI; **customer satisfaction, retention and conquest
customers**; **staff satisfaction** – if the brand champions
aren't happy you are in trouble.

14 **A detailed business plan covering all the key financials**.
This part needs to be 'rock solid'. Do not do this alone. This is
where the best finance guy you can find or have in the
company is vital. It requires numbers against every activity –
welcome to the world of total measurement. It needs sales
numbers by category, investment by category, resource by
category, profit contribution by category. It's quite trying, but
be patient and play the game. The more ways that you can
move the numbers around, the happier the bean counters will
be. And always include a sensitivity analysis based on a number
of what-if scenarios focusing on levels of ROI. Include charts,
histograms – the whole bit. Sorry, but this is the 'asking for
money bit' and it needs to look really impressive and be very
comprehensive.

15 **The 'how will it be done'**.

a) step-by-step and detailed description of all aspects of the
strategic plan – the route map

● What is intended to be achieved analysed by all the key

▶

> marketing categories with numbers and broad
> descriptions?
>
> ● Focus on all the aspects of competitive, customer and
>   trade impact.
>
> **b)** and next you need to include detailed descriptions of all the
>   tactical ways the strategic plan will be achieved – the
>   modes of transport to be used in getting to your
>   destination.
>
> ● Detailed activity-by-activity descriptions covering all key
>   issues – why it's being done, what the effect will be.
>
> ● An 'activity map' which identifies all activities over time
>   with costs and people resource attached to them.
>
> ● A plan of how to 'sell' the tactical plan internally so it's
>   understood, bought into, applauded and how it is to be
>   delivered.
>
> **16 Credentials of all the key team** so anyone who looks at this
>   plan can have confidence that they can deliver it. This is so
>   important. If you don't have all the people you need on board
>   suggest how you will get them, how long it will take or
>   alternatively how you propose to recruit freelance talent.
>
> **17** If investors don't think you have the resource and talent
>   available now, they won't invest in it, however good the plan
>   looks.

Dressing the plan

This is all about presentation and the following tips could make
you a millionaire or leave you very, very disappointed if you
don't bother.

If you want to sell the plan, do the following:

1 Make sure it looks good with lots of relevant visual content – pie charts, histograms, easy-to-read tables and so on.

2 Make sure the typeface is large enough to read easily.

3 Avoid spelling mistakes.

4 Make sure it is bound and protected with an acetate cover.

5 Leave white space available for the recipient to make notes – this is after all a working document.

6 Make sure the author details – address, email – and date are clearly included.

7 It needs to look carefully, thoughtfully and thoroughly prepared but it must not look flashy.

8 The final acid test: does it convincingly present the argument?

9 Have you got the executive summary in a form that really sells the plan?

10 Have you got a PowerPoint presentation that does justice to the plan and which you can give at a moment's notice? Presentation matters in the modern world. Please take it seriously.

brilliant tip

Ask a colleague whose judgement you trust to go through the plan and your presentation of it, focusing on uncovering any obvious weaknesses. Health checks are always to be recommended.

The importance of planning

Yes, marketing plans take a long time and are tiresomely full of hard questions. But it's worth it, because if you go through the process you will, indeed, become quite quickly a world expert in your brand and how to make it succeed. Not only will you have the journey and the route map completely worked out but you will also be brilliantly equipped to cope with all the challenges anyone on a journey might encounter from economic storms to competitive ambushes.

One thing will become apparent to you as you go through this process. Simplicity is a virtue. Too many plans are too complex and too clever. Brilliant marketing is about taking the quickest, safest and most economic route from A to Z. But most of all, constructing a really robust and impressive marketing plan is exciting as it takes you deep into the engine room of competitive marketing.

Good luck.

CHAPTER 20

How to choose and manage suppliers, agencies and brilliant people

A word about talent

Talent has never been easy to find or manage. Marketing people are very often that infuriating blend of very charming, very opinionated and very stubborn. At their best they trade in a quasi-creative world that involves a lot of numbers and some sometimes quite wacky ideas. I once heard of someone who wanted their marketing for a brand of milk to be 'dangerous' – what was that all about? The tension between right and left brain is very apparent with talented marketers. And while some may not find them easy, the difference they can make to sales and profit makes them pretty useful members of any business team.

Brilliant people

I've worked with many companies – from Heinz, through the government departments – some six of them – to Guinness, Panasonic, Mazda, Ford, Lucas, Bulmers. And I've also worked in or with about 11 advertising agencies. So I've seen real talent, blooming talent, burnt-out talent, idiots and geniuses, gypsies, vagabonds and the whole lot. On reflection there was more talent than the reverse and more evidence of bad management than bad people.

Most people want to do good work. It's a brilliant end product, not just money, that drives most of the people I've worked with.

Choosing the right people

There are four rules.

1   Do they pass the Nottingham Monday test? It's 7.30am on a Monday and you are going to Nottingham. Do you think you'd be glad to have them as a travelling companion? If the answer is 'no' or 'not sure' they should not be hired.

2   Do not mistake talent on paper for talent in the flesh. I've so often seen great CVs produced by people who are less impressive when you meet them.

3   First impressions are critical and if someone doesn't pass that test then forget about them, but that first meeting alone creates only one dimension. What you should do is create a lot of first impressions by seeing a prospective work colleague – either an employee or a supplier – a lot of times before you finally make your mind up. We know that anyone who works for Google is interviewed up to twenty times.

> first impressions are critical but that first meeting creates only one dimension

4   Do not work with a lot of clones of yourself. What you need are people who share your values and culture but who think differently. The best combination is when an intellectual chemistry is achieved which is symbiotic. We all know that there are people that bring out the best in us. Go and find them.

Finding the right people in life is a key to success, especially in marketing, where having a real human touch and where having people who can influence others and change minds is so important. The right way to find these people is by being as sociable a person as possible. The more people you meet the better your antennae become at identifying stronger and weaker potential candidates.

If you are part of an organisation find the best people in HR and cultivate them. In my experience good HR people are terrific at spotting talent. If, on the other hand, you are working alone and have no access to HR professionals, do two things:

● apply the rule of four (see above) rigorously;

● take your time. Choosing people with whom you are going to share your marketing project is a commitment as critical as making a big financial commitment like buying a house or a car.

Choosing professional suppliers

The same rules apply, but the impact of a wrong decision when appointing a marketing services agency can be very expensive and career damaging. Let's face it though, the people who work in advertising and PR are pretty good at selling themselves, so it can be hard to distinguish the great from the not so great or, even more importantly, the great people from the right people.

The different kinds of agency need explaining as there are so many different specialists around. The key ones that have very specific skills are advertising agencies, PR consultancies, media planning and buying agencies, sponsorship consultancies, design companies, digital agencies, marketing consultancies and, quite recently, a number of experiential marketing agencies have been set up. What do you need? It depends on what you need to achieve, but it's likely that at the outset an advertising agency and a PR consultancy will serve you best and act as conduits to other disciplines.

| follow the talent and the integrity |

My number one rule of life is to follow the talent and the integrity. If you are lucky enough to find someone who has both use them as an adviser – they'll save you time, money and heartache in helping you select what you really need.

So how do you proceed? Well, if you know absolutely nothing about this marketplace you have to learn something first, otherwise you may be taken to the cleaners. Agencies may say they want your business, are passionate to work on this fascinating challenge ... but let's also be clear – they really want your money.

Building an agency shortlist

You are looking to create a shortlist of no more than four agencies and you'll have to reconcile yourself to the fact this will take some time – maybe as much as 100 hours in total, so do not embark on it lightly. To find out more do six things:

- Read a few copies of *Campaign*, *Marketing Week* and *PRWeek*. These are available in most libraries and certainly business libraries like that in the Institute of Directors. Begin to get a feeling for the landscape.

- Go to Business Link www.businesslink.gov.uk which will be helpful. The best operator around is the Advertising Agency Register www.aargroup.co.uk who cover all kinds of agencies but are not cheap; www.thedrum.co.uk is an online publication useful for agencies outside London.

- Talk to as many people you can find who use agencies and ask them about their experiences and about the agencies that are currently doing the most effective work. And if I were an agency I'd be running free courses on how to choose an agency and manage a relationship – it seems so obvious doesn't it?

● Look at as many pieces as possible of PR coverage, advertising campaigns and so on, and if you like something find out who did it and write to them or phone them and ask them all about it. Try to gauge their enthusiasm and intellect.

● Finally here's the start of a useful checklist – add to it but refer to it assiduously if you decide you need to create a shortlist of agencies, bearing in mind that in using an agency, unless you choose someone hopelessly wrong, you'll get a much better job than if you do it yourself.

i) How much money do you have to spend? Unless you are in the top five or six clients in an agency question whether you will get the attention you want or think you deserve. When you hear an agency you like has just won Vodafone or Sainsbury's wonder if this will be good for little old you if you appoint them.

ii) Is this a new or an existing brand or service? Also is it a trophy brand like Innocent or an unknown like Barkham garden tools? Deciding on the task that needs doing is key. Some people are great at launching things, others at building brands over time.

iii) What do you believe you need and in roughly what proportion – advertising, PR, design, direct marketing, digital? If you don't know do not go shopping, because you'll be liable to do the equivalent of going to a garden centre when what you really need is a pair of trousers. Maybe you need a marketing consultant. Call Business Link or, better still, get back to work on that marketing plan and work it out.

iv) What sort of people do you want to work with? Go back to the Rule of Four. Bear in mind that you must insist the person you find whom you want to work on your business is guaranteed to work on it – you can have this inserted into any contract with the agency you choose. Also bear in mind that this is a business of teams and individuals. The actual firm you choose is far less important than the people who'll work on your business.

v) Time spent on reconnaissance is rarely wasted . . . start to visit agencies for short periods – say a succession of half-hour meetings with those agencies who have interested you. Always arrive too early and say, 'I'm OK, leave me here I have calls to make.' Use the time in reception to get a flavour of the company. The reception is very often the hub of the whole place.

vi) Do not do this by yourself (unless there is only you). Try to travel in convoy because as a team you will be more observant than by yourself.

Choosing a shortlist of agencies

You and your team should have decided the agencies who you think could do a good job for you.

Be ruthless about omitting firms too big, too busy, too complacent, too arrogant, too young, too old, too servile and so on from your list.

Be sure to talk to some of the clients of those agencies (who are a similar size to you) whom you are thinking of putting on your list, to find out what they are good at and not so good at as a whole, and specifically to find out more about the people who'll work on your business. The acid questions will always be these:

- Are they good enough to solve my problems?
- Can we work together?
- Will my business be important enough for them?
- Are they creative enough to multiply my money?

Giving them a brilliant brief

I've shown you how to produce a great brief but you need to add two elements: what you and your team expect from an agency ... regard this as 'marriage vows' – no I'm not fooling around; and vice versa – what the agency expects from a client. Chances are they've never written this down before. To work this has to be a partnership so what do they want from you to operate at their best?

You need to work with each agency, making sure they really understand the brief and that you really understand the way they work and think. In fact plan to spend at least a few hours working with them before any formal pitch so you can get a very clear view as to what it would be like if you actually appointed them. Whatever you do, do not pin everything on the pitch itself – people have on days and off days – you want to know about weeks not days.

At this early stage make them want to work with you so you get the opportunity to see them at their best.

Running a perfect pitch

Be even-handed.

Cut each agency enough slack to be themselves and maybe blow your mind by doing some really creative and unusual stuff. It's not a bad idea if you are very busy to appoint an external manager to co-ordinate the whole process.

Alternatively run a pitch process in which each agency has two hours including Q&A, that these pitches are back to back over two days and that the pitch itself is worth 60 per cent of the marks awarded (all the pre-work you do with them comprises the other 40 per cent) and the score sheet comprises the following:

- Chemistry with you***
- How smart**
- How creative**
- How responsive*
- How good at listening*
- How confident
- How good at making connections between things
- How strong as a team
- Quality of agency leadership
- How efficient.

(* = absolutely critical criteria)

The reason for being so prescriptive about this is to ensure you really think through a critical partnership appointment from both points of view – yours and theirs.

Tell them you'll inform them of your decision within one week of the pitch (and do so) or if you need more information ask for it within that week. Understand that waiting to hear if you've won or not is very stressful.

Managing the agency relationship

There is indeed a magic cocktail. It's about making them (the agencies) desperate to make you succeed and never settling for second best; for them to assume quasi-ownership of your business; for you to acquire brand leadership in their mind – so they are working for you even when they are asleep. In my life the Department of Health, Heinz, Guinness, Lucas, Watneys and Bulmers all did this.

Clever investment

We'd had a chunk of Heinz business for a while when they called and said they wanted to meet me. My heart sank (paranoia in agencies is never far from the surface). They walked in and said, 'We want to thank you for doing a great job and we'd like to take the agency on a magical mystery tour which I'm afraid will involve a large amount of alcohol.'

Result? Team in love with Heinz (once the hangover went) = client gets extra super service.

Four words define a business love affair. These are they. THANK YOU. WELL DONE.

brilliant tip

It is time buyers in service businesses recognised that they should and must be more demanding, but always with humour and always (without fail) with courtesy.

Rule of life: People who like you will try harder for you.

Summary

1 Choose people you like, respect and trust whose work you admire.

2 Always sort out the money early on. Is it a fixed monthly retainer? Is there a variable element? Sort it out – this is business.

3 Do the agency understand what you as a business are trying to achieve – all of them, not just the main contact?

4 Do the agency understand the competitive world in which you live with all its complexities?

5 Are they real experts on your own brand?

6 Are you getting enough of their thinking time?

7 Are they responsive and efficient in reporting back?

8 Are you fast in registering pleasure and the reverse?

9 Are they hitting agreed targets? If not, what are they doing to remedy this?

10 Are they astute about money and operating to budget? Are you satisfied they are on top of this?

11 Is there a stability of relationship in terms of your key contacts?

12 Are they capable of staying on their game and remaining creative and smart? And is there a mechanism for you to make sure they know (immediately) if they start to slide backwards?

Conclusion: an agency relationship is like a marriage

There are only two words to say. These are:

'I do.'

And then go off and do it, on a bed of trust, ambition and enthusiasm.

CHAPTER 21

The ten ways to manage a marketing campaign

Time to worry – you have the 'green light'

So the marketing plan has been approved. In fact it's been received with a huge level of enthusiasm. You and the team are very pleased. Or, if this is you by yourself, you are elated to have got such praise from your investors. But it's that three o'clock in the morning time when you realise words on paper and deeds in the real world are not the same . . . Now you have to make it all happen.

The ten ways to be a brilliant campaign manager

1 **Be visible. Stand up and 'champion' the cause.**

There is nowhere to hide. This is your plan and quite rightly you have to own it, be responsible for it, speak for it and about it. Until the campaign has been successfully launched and starts to deliver results you are going to spend most of your life thinking about it and worrying about it. You are an architect watching your carefully thought through building going up.

2 **Make the team meet weekly. Have morning catch-ups. Checklists are key.**

Details are key. Rhetoric is a heady kind of fuel but we are in the business of constantly making sure everything is in

team meetings are vital

the right place at the right time. Welcome to project management. The team meetings are vital. Make sure everyone knows exactly what is expected of them. Keep on chasing. Take absolutely nothing for granted. It makes complete sense to have a daily check-up, especially in the early days of the campaign. Embed urgency, a sense of curiosity and an obsession with delivery, results and measurement into the campaign.

3 **Have diverse opinion.**

It's easy, running a campaign in this way, for the team to become so focused that they stop listening to contrary opinion. It is absolutely critical that you have a weekly team meeting where you get a real diversity of view expressed by people in the call centres, in the sales team, in the manufacturing unit. The bigger, the more constantly involved and more diverse the team, the better the chance of being able to make necessary modifications to the plan as and when necessary.

4 **You need a fact monitor – a person who captures everything going on.**

Even the simplest of campaigns needs to have someone who is tracking everything, who keeps the paper trail under control. The worst examples of error and monetary waste come when the expression 'but I thought . . . ' is heard. The person heading up the campaign (unless there is no one else) should not be the one who is secretary of the event as well – too much information and too much vested interest in one head. But if you are on your own, keep track of things in one book, but by all means transfer to your PC as you go.

5 Get out and look at things yourself – what others say is not enough.

Seeing people buying your product in the shops or looking at it and not buying it may teach you more than anything else. Marketing campaigns are real, expensive and noisy things that are designed to create momentum and actually make something happen. Field trips, as these tours out into the real battleground are known, are never wasted experiences.

6 Change things if they aren't working – crisis meetings are good.

As my experience has grown I have become more sceptical about the all singing, all dancing launch. Way back when big companies had huge sales forces the dramatic launch event may have made sense. I recall two – one flying the length of Britain in a private plane so salesmen could be addressed at three different locations on the same day, ensuring they were out selling equipped with the new sparkling campaign the next day. The other transmitting a spoof *News at Ten* at ten in the morning on the ITV network to the Bulmers' sales team throughout the UK. We used the presenters as they then were, Andrew Gardner and Reginald Bosanquet, to describe a new campaign for cider. Newsy. A first. And it stuck in the mind. These were expensive and, in retrospect, quite high risk activities. Potentially a Terminal 5 moment. I much prefer lower key events in the expectation that things will be changed as one goes along, making that big fanfare redundant. Better by far to have that big party when the campaign has succeeded. Crisis meetings and a touch of Dunkirk is excellent because it produces a lot of useful

do not be sentimental. If something isn't working change it

adrenalin. By the way do not be sentimental. If something isn't working change it.

7 Expect feedback from the market/media/internal the whole time – do not wait.

You will have built a constant feedback system so you hear exactly what is going on the whole time. It is your job to anticipate and, in so far as is possible, control the stories that occur in the media and internally. You will have a series of milestones planned, but will also be nimble enough to take advantage of any opportunities that arise to add velocity to the campaign by doing unplanned media interviews. Most of all, you must become measurement obsessed. Your job is to track exactly what is going on and what is changing in the market. There are no prizes for ignorance.

8 Be one team – have constant co-ordination.

The power of a co-ordinated team can be awesome. It is critical that you make sure everyone on the team is constantly updated and involved. 'Nobody told me . . . ' are words that can never be uttered in a properly run team. These constant meetings, phone calls and emails are designed to maintain maximum and constant alignment. Go to Google and they call their teams 'huddles'. There the team owns a project and has power to do what it takes to make a project succeed. I've never felt so much band-of-brothers alignment anywhere else.

9 Celebrate success and failure – this is a curve of learning how to succeed.

Do not underestimate the motivational impact of celebrating success. You can't do it every day, but what you must do is make everyone feel they are part of a winning team. You see this in Formula One to an exaggerated extent. You saw it in banking when banks were winning. But if something goes wrong (and it will) prove that you are not part of a blame culture by getting everyone together to explore how to solve it there and then. You are going to be a supreme execution machine and that means solving issues and applauding effective action. It means being fast.

10 Support the team. Love the team. Grow the team.

I know Harriet Jones at McCann Erickson, the advertising agency, becomes rather misty-eyed when she talks about her team. Certainly there is something impressive about a bunch of people working together with their egos firmly parked. The keys are that the leaders and all the members of the team have to support each other, respect each other and watch each other's talents develop and flourish. This is Godfather time. You are in this together. One of the best examples I've seen of a campaign team at work was when the team at Heinz launched Weight Watchers from Heinz Frozen Ready Meals. Amazing work ethic; terrific sense of bonding; great fun.

A winning campaign takes a lot of management

If you've ever worked on a great campaign you'll know it's a little like the theatre – late nights, lots of rehearsing, occasional improvisation, changes to the script as it goes along, elation and disappointment. There's a sense of being very, very close to the trees and not being able to see the wood.

Make sure you have your own 'inspirers' on whom you can call. There are no medals for trying to do too much yourself. Just occasionally you need a sympathetic and a brilliant pat on the back.

I can recall (and some may find this surprising) just how brilliant the government used to be at creating a real sense of team. The civil servants I worked with were very impressively collegiate.

brilliant tip

Never underestimate the amount of time that management takes.
Brilliant marketing needs more than money and resources. It
requires the leadership of a general, the patience of a gardener, the
agility of an ice skater and the sense of humour of a professional
comedian.

PART 4

Strategy, creativity and the bigger picture

When sophisticated techniques and concepts come into play

The future and how you can be a key part of it

CHAPTER 22

Sorry, there's been a budget cut

All about money

I n the current economic climate money is tight. No, start again. Money is always tight and everyone in marketing should expect budgetary restraint as a norm. The so-called tensions between the finance and marketing functions are the normal tensions that exist where hard and searching questions are asked about ROI. And it's got a little more complicated now because increasingly CFOs have got more sophisticated and able to understand the way marketing works and the

> everyone in marketing should expect budgetary restraint as a norm

way marketers feel about their plans (which they ought to regard as their babies – so do not DARE criticise the advertising or the plan. It is sacrosanct!).

Ultimately, business is about generating more money than we spend and ensuring what we do spend is well and prudently spent. Owing to the pressure to spend well and almost certainly find savings during the year, any smart marketer is going to be well versed in how to save money and perhaps, even more importantly, how to defend critical areas of the plan.

Be transparent

Make sure whoever it is that is funding your marketing investment (CFO, CEO, bank manager, dragon, angel, v.c., private equity, you and your wife's joint account) is given the courtesy of proper explanation and presentation so before the event they know pretty well exactly what they are in for. This will save much angst and confusion later on.

Be calm

This is business, as Don Corleone quipped. It calls for reason, clarity and focus. Do not be overly protective. Try to be dispassionate. There is a lot of talk about 'passion' in business. Passion does not belong in a conversation about money, especially when someone is trying to take it away.

Avoid waste

Marketing is a bit like a fuel-thirsty car revving up with a Ferrari-like exhaust at the traffic lights. It consumes forests of documents, electricity bills of PowerPoint presentations, travel and entertainment is a well-thumbed expense category ('no stranger to the mini-bar were we?). Just determine to be careful on every item of expenditure. Become a new puritan.

Get it right the first time

The downside of the endless quest for perfection is that money flows away on projects that are refined and re-refined. Spend more time asking all the questions before you spend any money. There is more waste in marketing than you'd see in a middle-class refrigerator. Don't spend a penny until you know where you are going and when.

Do a theoretical exercise privately

On the basis that a budget cut is almost inevitable, prepare 'private' plans B, C, D, E which envisage how you'd respond to a series of different budget cuts. Cutting budget may be the necessity demanded by the CEO, but they don't expect this to be accompanied by a 'but we'll miss the plan by a mile now' response. You a marketer – how do you fix the sort of problem you're liable to be served up?

Become more ROI obsessed than the finance people

The name of the game is 'what-do-I-spend-what-do-I-get?' And if you aren't completely fixated on answering this question you have a problem. Assuming you are now in the mood to say sardonically to your CFO 'you finance people treat money so much more lightly than we do, possibly because you are used to bigger numbers, but every penny I spend hurts unless I can see the return coming in', seriously keep on asking the question about everything – your marketing activity, your agencies, your people – 'Am I getting the most I could out of them?'

Could you really buy better?

Well of course you could. You can get rid of people; you can negotiate harder; you can demand a Tesco Value sort of service. But the issue is can you get better results for less money? Can you make £1 work like £10? This is all about relationships and unselfishly understanding the needs of all your suppliers.

How many people could you save?

No, I haven't gone religious. You and I may be these 'people' and save is a euphemism for 'fire'. Examine this equation. If only I could motivate my people so they worked say 15 per cent more productively; if only I could get people to work longer hours – say an extra hour a day; if only I could simplify the tasks so we focused harder on less, then ... you'd be able to get by on 25 per cent fewer people. Another way of looking at the same equation is to ask if this is really so, whether you could improve your performance by between a quarter and a third with what you've got. No one likes firing people so it's time to be more ambitious in your targets.

How do you handle variable workload?

Freelance. This is when getting in real, temporary, expensive talent really pays for itself. Make sure you have a list of competent people who can help out. Many of these are brilliant young mothers who can work from home.

Spread versus depth

If your budget has been ravaged by a blunder elsewhere in the business or simply through economic circumstances, consider a radical rewrite of the plan (plan F). Never buy a ticket halfway to New York – you'll end up in the sea – just revise your budget with this in mind. Consider maintaining the quantity of impact against a smaller universe. Better by far to prove your plan works than the original plan reduced in investment doesn't. A no brainer that.

Can you refine your target market?

This is where the mathematician media planners come in, or failing that or being unable to afford them you need to review your target market. The most important people are those who bought from you before. But the basic rule of thumb is this – define who you want to talk to much more precisely than you have done so far and you can save a lot of money. 'I want to talk to everyone' is a very expensive wish indeed.

> the most important people are those who bought from you before

You must build in a contingency

Never produce a budget without a contingency line in it. And then, on a line by line basis, maintain a small contingency sum which is not notional but actual. Something which, if push came to shove, you could save without wrecking the overall plan and which you'll probably save anyway. Building a budget, guarding it and saving sums within it are all part of the skills of being a brilliant marketer. Do not, however, be affronted when they want money back halfway through the year ... help them, but make sure this hasn't meant you've had to sit up all night working out how on earth to do it.

brilliant tip

Find a friend or a colleague who is very financially astute who can help you through all this. While they do the maths you can drink wine and be creative.

Conclusion

Managing money matters. The task of a great marketer is to deliver results and to create a plan that does that. But money is the root of all marketing plans, so you have to be great at the money, not just at the creativity.

managing money matters

CHAPTER 23

The art of creative thinking – turning brilliance into reality

What is creativity?

We hear a lot about creativity in business nowadays (almost as much as we hear about passion in business.) The trouble is that very few understand what creativity is and even fewer know how to be creative. There is no adequate scientific definition of it. There is some bizarre impression that impulsive and random non sequiturs may be creative; that you have to be crazy to be creative. In fact, despite impressions to the contrary, the art of creativity lies in making connections, in cross-referencing ideas so people start to think in a different way. Creativity is about being relaxed enough to have lots of ideas, not just one great one. But the real art is in getting rid of the rubbish.

Let's be creative (a parable that's sadly commonplace)

Gilbert surveyed his colleagues gloomily. Matthew had trousers that were ankle flappers and a badly creased cardigan, Hector was overweight and wheezing – too many cigarettes thought Gilbert – so old-fashioned a habit – probably drinks pale ale too. Maureen was quite pretty or would have been if she hadn't insisted on wearing a micro-skirt, fishnet stockings, pigtails and dark glasses. 'OK team', said Gilbert, 'we've been asked to be creative in finding ways to increase the sales of Vegebix. Every department's involved.

▶

It's the new CEO's idea – you know the things he's been saying – 'we want to help all the staff, not just the marketing guys, to think more creatively each day' – well this is Project Unleash. So let's get creative.

There was an immediate and horrified response. Matthew broke wind, Hector burst into a coughing fit and Maureen uncrossed her legs (ooh, I do wish she wouldn't do that).

'Right, spluttered Gilbert, wishing he had a more convincing set of subordinates. 'Here's what we do. We need to do something that seizes people's attention. We need to repackage the product so it has stand-out. How about putting it in a Bird's Eye plastic frozen pea type pack with great big vegetable shots, carrots, parsnips and aubergine all standing very erect in a priapian way, get it displayed in the chilled cabinet, change the name to Power-Crunch Vegebix©, write masses of blogs and so on about "how it's ruined my wife's sleep pattern, with me wanting to embark on sexual marathons because of all that veggie power . . . I mean don't talk to me about your five-a-day, watch out for five a night" – and the team can all dress up as vegetables offering samples around and shouting the new Vegebix slogan – 'Weyhay! Weyhay! Get some today.' And we could have a vegetable parade going down every high street in the country with people chanting something like, 'Have your veg, get your fix. Feel much better with Vegemix. Have your fix, have your lunch, get the power of Power-Crunch. How does that sound team?' They glanced nervously at each other and then at Gilbert. Hector coughed. 'Why don't we just do a BOGOF* boss?'

(* Buy one get on free – much favoured by salesmen as a way of driving volume.)

So much for creativity.

Why creativity is so key

At the very heart of brilliant marketing are a series of ingredients, but most of all and most excitingly, a creative idea, something that is in some way inspirational, different and which catapults the objective you've set yourself into engaging and real action. Most of all it is likely to create momentum, a sense of something changing. We are talking about innovation. Something that is a catalyst to change in some way. Creativity lies in words like Martin Luther King's 'I have a dream' or a logo like 'I ♥ America' or a picture like that little girl fleeing the bombs in Vietnam. Shame that such a sight could be called creative, but it did the most creative thing that can be done. It changed minds.

Left brain. Right brain

David Heslop, one time CEO of Mazda and Expotel, is now involved in a company called Sospiro (Italian for 'Sigh') which coaches senior executives to get their brain in tune. The argument goes that years ago, in the more literary world, we were more right-brained and intuitive, that as the Age of Art moved to the Age of Science – basically in the late nineteenth and early twentieth centuries – we became left-brained, which was fine then but isn't now, because what we need in this Age of Knowledge and Communication is to be more intuitive again – what David describes as a migration from a 'think-do' world to a 'do-think' world.

The coaching programmes are crammed with real-time compositions of music and plays – creative events which apparently change people's lives. What intrigues me is the fact that there are certain pre-conditions to be creative:

● a right brain on red alert

- a fully attuned sense of curiosity
- a lot of material to play with – don't tell me a blank sheet of paper is a good thing
- a sense of the need to produce something – deadlines are great goads
- laughter.

brilliant tip

Always listen to your inner voice (you may have 500 reasons to do something but if your heart isn't saying 'yes' don't do it).

What Stanford University taught us

Professor Michael Ray, the John G. McCoy-BancOne Corporation Professor of Creativity and Innovation and Marketing, Emeritus, is a phenomenon who has changed a lot of lives. His course at Stanford, which he ran with Rochelle Myers, is spoken of with awe by those who've been on it. His advice is simplistic:

- be yourself in life
- take a deep breath and ask yourself 'yes' or 'no' – often the answer simply comes to you
- *'Do only what is easy, effortless and enjoyable'* – that's Jim Collins, author of *From Good to Great*, who went on the course in 1983 – yes, it's been going that long
- your life is a work of art and the kind of creativity he teaches is essential to health, success and happiness in life, in business and above all in marketing.

It sounds a bit mystical but what is so appealing about all this is that Michael is an obvious and keen student of human nature and the positivism (unless you are a Van Gogh or a Proust) that leads to great and life-changing creativity for marketers. The key for any great marketing is to understand who the target is, where they are at, what is likely to engage them and why they may be reached by what

> marketing at its most brilliant is not a craft or a science. Brilliant marketing is an art

you have to tell them. But it is not just about a transfer of information, because marketing at its most brilliant is not a craft or a science. This is the big lesson here. Brilliant marketing is an art.

Ted Nierenberg, founder of Dansk International Design, said this:

'The uncreative life isn't worth living.'

I'm with Ted.

Creativity is high on the political agenda too

In a report recently published by the Department of Culture, Media and Sport, it was concluded:

'The challenge is to create a culture in higher education that links creativity with innovation of creative value.'

I love the sang-froid of government. This is more than words-on-a-page challenge. It's a mighty adventure that needs massive funding. Trouble with government. All talk. No walk. All mouth and trousers.

In recent times, the number of creative businesses (62,000) in the UK has been growing rapidly (by 40 per cent over a five-year period). The skills in managing creativity are improving, but too slowly. Too many of us regard the need to do things on time and on budget as more important than doing things brilliantly. Sir Jeremy Isaacs (ex head of Channel 4 and the Royal Opera House, and no slouch when it came to managing creativity) said in the *Financial Times* in 1999 these timeless words:

'Your prime role as a manager is enabling creativity to fulfil itself.'

Vodafone did a piece of research in 2005 which encouragingly (well, I think it's encouraging) showed the following:

- 28 per cent of their employees had at least one new idea a week
- two-thirds believed their managers were likely to listen to new ideas
- in companies where no inducement or reward structure was in place just under a third of people never had an idea.

But it cannot simply be planned – 'today I shall be creative' – you can try it, but don't hold your breath. Amin Rajan, CEO of Create, a research company, put it rather well when he described creativity in an organisation as 'a random explosion born out of frustration with the status quo'. Creativity matters so much because it is there to facilitate and drive change. And creativity is vital in marketing, where the key aims in the quest for brilliance are as follows:

- to be noticed
- to change opinion
- or to strengthen opinion
- to provoke action.

Learning how to be creative

Claire Sparks of Shine Communications talks about the need to be inspired by feeding her mind and there, in one leap, Claire has nailed the core truth about creativity. Unless you have that unquenchable appetite for the new, different and extraordinary, chances are you won't be able to join the creative club.

So how do you get into the creative zone? Here's a ten-point programme which can begin to turn you from a corporate duckling into a suave creative swan.

1 Creative identity

Think about two ways of introducing yourself to a room of people – the safe way and the dramatic way. *'My name is Richard Hall. I have worked in marketing, advertising, leadership and coaching roles . . . ' . . .* zzzzzzzzzzzzzzz

Or *'What on earth was I thinking about giving up a nice solid job as a client to join the debauchery of advertising?' . . .* Hmm. More promising.

2 Choosing creativity.

Visit a shop and seek out two things you think are really creative and decide exactly why you think that is . . . find two things, by the same token, you think are boring.

3 Thinking about creativity.

Now do the same thing with two different kinds of art – you define what art is – and yes it could be an ad. But they must be different – music and poetry; a painting and a play. Ask yourself just why they stand out. Also question why you like them and see how much you can find to say about them that is interesting or relevant.

4 Journeys into creativity.

Now go on a journey – first of all a short one, walking down a high street near where you live with a camera, taking pictures of anything that strikes you as interesting. Try and create a story around the ten most interesting pictures and how they enable you to describe the way the world is changing and what's going to happen next.

Now go on a longer journey. Preferably go through an airport. Think about what you'd change. Imagine you were appointed Lord High Executioner with absolute powers. So what would you get rid of and what would you add? And when you get to where you are going, what are the three most important things that are different?

5 **Creative abundance.**

Don't be suckered into believing during the creative process that less is more. Less is less. You need to fill pages, walls, rooms and mansions with your stuff. Prolific is good. Take a product, any product but especially, for preference, one you like and write down in a couple of hours on a big A2 pad as many different marketing ideas that might increase sales. Be as wild and wacky as you like. Then spend an hour picking the half-dozen or so which seem to have the most promise, and then spend an hour polishing those so they have a veneer of thoughtfulness and zing. This exercise is designed to get your creative juices flowing not to produce a great marketing campaign. It's designed to produce an answer to the question, 'Can you create stuff?' Because if you can you'll have a brilliant time. At first you'll find some of the ideas aren't that good, but the more you are producing – in general – the better they'll get.

6 **Creative teams.**

This is where it gets a bit trickier. Fact is $1 + 1 = 3$. Yes – synergy applies. That's why you have creative teams in advertising agencies who are both copywriters and art directors – their roles often cross over. Try working with a kindred spirit whose opinion and creativity you respect. See if between you you can produce more and better thinking than just you alone. I am not talking about you producing ads, just broad-scale thinking on marketing issues and the beginnings of a marketing plan.

7 **Fast forward creativity.**

Occasionally in a crisis you need to be able to come up with a bunch of creative options in very little time. Let us suppose you have a product recall – how do you minimise the damage and maximise the opportunities when you are back on course again. ('Why don't we do a BOGOF boss?' Maybe that is the right answer . . . maybe. But let's have a series of options.) Let's suppose you hear a competitor is about to launch a well-priced product which competes with your main profit earner; or that you are gaining share and losing sales – in other words the market is declining. This is all exciting stuff that needs exciting responses. Brilliant marketing requires original, creative thinking. It also requires fast response.

> brilliant marketing requires original, creative thinking

8 **Mobilising crisis-creativity.**

This is when you have a real need to integrate everything – it's probably a specific challenge with which you have to deal. The idea is a development of R.H. Schaffer and General Electric's 'Work Out' programme, and relies on the basic truth that those who do the work usually know better how to improve the way they do it than those who manage them. So get a whole bunch of front-line operators – people in call centres, your PR company, your advertising agency, your receptionists, sales people, your finance people and so on – in a room, say (depending on the size of your company) seven people in each group. For a few hours get them to debate a couple of specific challenges and get them to report back their solutions. You'll be amazed how brilliant they are.

9 **Take lots of baths.**

No, I'm not being flippant. It wasn't just Archimedes who found baths useful. In a world of showers our creativity is under severe threat – so get in that bath and let your mind roam. And you also need to take intellectual baths by doing things your consumers might do, from watching *Coronation Street*, to going to a football match, to watching *The Simpsons* film, watching Amy Winehouse or spending a night in a pub on quiz night. The key is to wash away the spread-sheet cobwebs that corrode marketing today; and if you want to be really inspired just look at YouTube and the best commercials. Pepsi – the Japanese Football ad, Peugeot 206 – the Indian ad, Adidas – the banned football ad (was it really banned?). I watched all of those and several others a few minutes ago and it was a brilliantly liberating experience. I really understood brilliant marketing in three dimensions. Try it.

10 **Meeting your consumers.**

And just maybe the most creative thing you can do is to have a series of focus groups – no, actually I don't mean focus groups – I mean getting a bunch of your consumers together and having a conversation with them – maybe even over a beer or a glass of wine. You'll learn a lot. You'll also have a lot of fun. And back to the old refrain – but worth repeating because it's so true:

You will never be brilliant at marketing unless you really get to know your consumers.

Do the above and you'll be much more creative than you've ever been before. You'll have lubricated your mind and started to think in a positively questioning way. But there's one other thing you have to do – become an avid student and aficionado of innovation.

brilliant examples of creativity

- **Prius** put solar panels in their car roofs. Why? Because they discovered a lot of their owners were prone to have a snooze in their car at lunchtime and wanted the air conditioning on but didn't want to leave the engine running. Brilliant thinking and so right for the brand.

- **Prêt-à-Porter at the Berkley Hotel**. They wanted to do something creative for ladies who'd lunched and now wanted to have tea but cucumber sandwiches were sooo not it. So the people at the Berkley created designer fashion biscuits with each designer contributing to the colour and shape of their own range. Talk of the tea set.

- **Boutique camping** – the progeny of years of Glastonbury. Really comfy tents that are brilliantly appointed. Luxury loo and shower blocks are now provided at key events. Sleeping in the open air is the new staying in a luxury ski chalet at Val d'Isère.

- **Two from M&S**. Airflex soles which are incredibly comfy and diminish foot odour in shoes. Sort of air-conditioning for feet. Then there's 'coin catcher' trousers which have pockets which are designed to stop your change falling out. My issue? It appears to me that they can't be bothered to market their creative innovations which seems most odd and really remiss as their marketing since the arrival of Steven Sharp has been brilliant.

Summary

We need to recognise that the chances of our regaining a manufacturing industrial base again are virtually non-existent, but that our opportunities as designers, inventors and simply as being cleverly creative are enormous. We need creative-ideas villages not business parks and we need a lot of them, so that one group's ideas can rub off on another's. And finally Tony Bair with a spot-on observation which endorses all this:

'*We are going to see the world economy dominated by the exploitation of creative minds.*'

What we nearly pulled off once in the financial services sector we really can pull off in creative services. And we must . . . so all you brilliant marketers out there – get to it.

CHAPTER 24

How to run a brilliant marketing workshop

Why marketing workshops are so important

'Talent wins games but teamwork and intelligence win championships.'

(Michael Jordan)

Workshops allow you and your colleagues to be creative and discover ways of marketing successfully that day to day stuck behind your PC, you might not achieve. Workshops are

workshops are the mechanism for unleashing competitive edge

the mechanism for unleashing competitive edge. Do not try to be a brilliant marketer by yourself – it won't work.

What is a workshop?

It's a group of colleagues who get together to thrash out a problem or series of problems or, alternately, try to work out how to realise one or more opportunities. It has as its guiding principle the belief that together we are stronger. But it stands or falls on how it's done.

Ingredients

One unusual and interesting venue.

One inspiring facilitator with an assistant or amanuensis (sorry, scribe or note taker), who can turn a mess into messages.

Eight to ten eager (getting people into the right frame of mind is critical) and very well-briefed participants representing different functions and skills.

Ten clear and carefully prepared briefing packs including a critical 'rules of engagement' or 'how we are going to cook this meal'.

At least three rooms so the group can be split up into two or three groups during the day.

At least (if possible) one overnight stay so the dish prepared can be reheated the next day and improved.

White boards and A2 easels with lots of paper and coloured marker pens.

Plenty of spice viz. stimuli for everyone – product samples, proto-types, competitors' samples, ads, PR releases, media coverage, videos, anything which puts the conversations that will be held into context.

Cooking instructions

Your master-chef-facilitator will lead this. She or he will have made sure everyone is brilliantly briefed and will have had a 121 with each beforehand. This is not a random exercise. It really needs great planning. The 121 will establish not the actual outcome, but the process, so that on the day every single mind is revving up to deliver its best.

The assistant/stand-in, apart from taking notes, makes sure everyone is comfortable and being treated properly. The minds in this room are valuable pieces of equipment and they deserve respect.

One other thing. There's one question the facilitators must keep asking the delegates and that is, 'What's missing?' Much better to ask this at the event than afterwards decide something was indeed missing but not mentioned.

The day/two-day programme will depend on the facilitator but will usually go through seven phases:

INTRODUCTION – who's who; why you are there; what you hope and expect to get out of it; the broad dimensions of the task.

INVESTIGATION – asking all the questions that need asking; making sure everyone has a clear handle on these issues; debating the scale of the challenge.

COMPLICATION – this is the messy bit, which is absolutely critical; try to raise and eliminate as many aspects of the challenge – all the problems, vested interests and detours; this is usually where everyone gets a bit grumpy and wonders where it's all going.

CREATION – a good period of time to be spent in smaller groups (two groups each with facilitators) on idea generation; create as many ideas as possible; work fast; work visually; be alive; have fun.

FOCUS – the editing process; the total group reconvenes and presents all the ideas to each other; reducing all the ideas down.

▶

This involves fast voting and absolutely needs consensus – no casting votes. You need to end up with no more than ten.

DEVELOPMENT – break off into groups of people with a few ideas for each group and develop and polish these so they have structure, life and the capacity to excite people. When you are happy, reconvene and refocus on the top five or six so you can improve them further.

ALIGNMENT – critical to end with an alignment session so everyone can feel they are on the same page and in overall commitment to the ideas you have. If possible see if you can reduce the ideas still further. Aim to have a synopsis of the workshop in bullet point form within two days to each delegate. A follow-up one-to-one between the facilitator and each delegate deters 'on second thoughts' misalignment.

The single most important objective of the workshop is that you come away with an agreed recipe for success or – and this sometimes happens – a recognition that there's something wrong with the recipe and it's back to the drawing board. This may be a really important discovery in itself and save a lot of money.

Post-prandial reflection

Workshops are brilliant places in which to sharpen a marketing campaign or solve a marketing issue. People together off-site tend to be more productive and more thoughtful.

Choice of location will depend on budget, but there are dozens of excellent country hotels you can find easily on the web. Just make sure the meeting rooms are good enough and that it will not be noisy at night.

The facilitator and the pre- and post-work she or he and their assistant do will pay you dividends although they increase the budget. But if you have no money you will have to think. For instance don't have an overnight stay; do it somewhere interesting but cheaper – the upstairs room in a pub; a meeting room in a local library; somewhere recommended by a local Chamber of Commerce or the Institute of Directors; and if it's summer you could even risk doing it outside. The key issue is to get the key people working together as a team and having the fun that the frisson of good challenging discussion has.

Who do you get to organise this?

If you have the budget there are a number of excellent people whom we can pass you to (www.richardhall.biz). You must be clear about what you want before anyone can be recommended with certainty. Do you want great facilitation or experienced participation in the discussion? If what you want is help on making sure you get the most out of such sessions over an extended period of time, save money and time by carefully selecting someone you trust or who is highly recommended and make their day by saying you'll have four or whatever of these over the next year.

brilliant tip

Quantity of preparation and quality of input will determine the quality of output.

The test of the recipe

Ask participants what they thought, and encourage constructive criticism.

Keep everyone involved with what happens as actions from the day are implemented or delayed or whatever.

Do NOT allow the day to be a 'team island' lost in a bureaucratic ocean – do not waste the momentum you achieved.

Never allow someone to come on a brainstorm or workshop for political reasons. It's the equivalent of putting chilli into a fish pie. Regard putting on a great workshop as the equivalent of putting on a great party. You want people to give a good time and have a good time and remember the event fondly in the future. And remember – to make workshops work you have to work at them.

to make workshops work you have to work at them

CHAPTER 25

Why research
can be a rude
word when
you are trying
to be brilliant

What is market research?

It is the technique of looking at and understanding customers' attitudes and their behaviour in all aspects of considering a brand. Research is about measuring and diagnosing. Research is your radar system. It is there to help you, not to make decisions for you. A good research insight can lead you to a brilliant place.

> research is there to help you, not to make decisions for you

 **example**

Two brilliant insights

My two favourite quotes on research are as follows:

'Most people use research much as a drunkard uses a lamp-post – more for support than illumination.'

(David Ogilvy)

'Using research to manage a business is like using the rear-view mirror to drive a car.'

(Dame Anita Roddick)

Always be cautious about science

We know that research is at best a pretty blunt tool, that stopping someone in the street and asking, 'What do you think of lavatory paper?' is unlikely to provoke a useful or even a truthful answer.

We have seen a diminishing credibility in the accuracy of political polls, with the remarkable exception of YouGov, due in part to its being completed privately as opposed to by a pollster, but more importantly than that because it is completed online. Doing things online tends to make you dispassionately honest in a way a normal questionnaire doesn't. An expert recently described the web as a 'disinhibiting environment'.

What's changed is that old-fashioned research is history

Learning about what consumers feel, think and do tells us about the past. This is critical in informing an understanding of the relationship between a brand and its consumer, but what is much less clear is how useful or informative asking consumers about something new and unknown like a new product or advertising can be.

Would we have had the fire or wheel if they had undergone market research?

The cavemen say 'no'

There was a series of films created by the Idea Group in San Diego about focus groups held with cavemen, first on fire, which to a Neanderthal they agreed would be better if it was cool – this is dangerous they mused – and if it were green and more symmetrical and not red-flamed, red was too aggressive a colour, reminiscent of blood and death . . . if there was a cool fire I might buy it, one said. So fire, as we know it, got the thumbs-down; as did the wheel, which they thought might run away downhill and hurt someone. So much better they agreed if it were square – much safer. Watch it – if nothing else puts you off badly run focus groups this will. http:// www.youtube.com/ watch?v=kuCAKuqRVQA. It's a brilliant little campaign, very funny and pointed, but most of all containing terrifying notes of truth.

Now go to YouTube, type in 'Focus Groups' and watch a few. You can't, first of all, distinguish between the parodies and the real thing. Housewives sitting around talking about the portion control cap on a premium salad dressing and worrying about things going wrong. I mean how likely are you to have salad dressing pouring everywhere from a normally capped bottle . . . but I suppose anything could happen . . .

Types of research

In simple terms there's quantitative research, which involves recruiting large panels of customers which can comprise:

- Ad hoc work to investigate a market
- Tracking studies (like Target Group Index or Taylor Nelson's shopper studies)
- Online research such as popularised by YouGov.com
- Brand purchase and stocking trends (Nielsen)
- Brand-switching studies started by AGB which show how many move brands, how often and when – a way of measuring the power of marketing activity
- Advertising research – day-after-recall work and effectiveness studies on a broader front done by people like Millward Brown
- Major government-funded social and economic studies

- Market studies like those produced by Mintel.

And there's qualitative research, which commonly comprises:

- Focus groups (or group discussions) usually lasting two hours and comprising a moderator with seven or so specially recruited respondents
- Depth interviews – one-to-one research work, typically an intensive hour's interview.

This is a big and complex field. Good research is expensive. Good researchers are often the brightest and most exciting intellects you'll encounter in marketing and tend to be adept at benchmarking things like advertising and new products. When a professional researcher says, 'In my experience' . . . it usually pays to listen.

Useful web sites. The Market Research Society, the market research national and international body, has two useful sites: www.mrs.org.uk and www.theresearchbuyersguide.com (I refer to this latter one later on).

More is more when it comes to learning

Years ago I went to an event called 'the big conversation' run by a clever ex-Unilever anthropologist called Dr Bart Sayle. The day consisted of 120 people or so, ordinary consumers, who spent two days in a London hotel talking to groups of guys from Guinness about the big issues regarding drinking. They thought women were badly treated by pubs and drinks manufacturers alike; there was little innovation in drink compared with say, food; the choice when it came to non-alcoholic drinks was laughable; men who drank too much confessed to not much liking themselves; everyone felt they were being short-changed when it came to social elegance because drinking inhabited a world of chipped glasses, puddles of booze, cigarette smoke, overflowing pints of lager, farts and belches; yet the big names in drinks, Stella, Heineken and Guinness, for instance, were, in contrast, quite sophisticated in their designs and advertising. They played around with this ambiguity with interest and decided there was a need for a rapid move upmarket, foretelling, as they did so, the emergence of gastro-pubs and wine bars like All Bar One.

A second example of 'more' was the Teutonic thoroughness with which the German confectioner August Storck KG prepared for the launch of Werther's Original in the UK. They asked for 150 depth interviews to be done – surely some kind of record. But the resultant launch was just brilliant – possibly one of the most brilliant FMCG (Fast Moving Consumer Goods) launches in the UK in the past 20 years.

Understanding what really matters

If I were a researcher I might be feeling a little fed up by now. This book claims to be about brilliance in marketing and yet here I have occasionally hinted that researchers are a cross between vandals, saboteurs and the Al Qaeda. (There are, I know, some creative people who'd say I was being too kind if I did say that. But I'm actually not saying it at all.)

Good, investigative research leads to discoveries like that Prius made about their solar panels and air-cooled snoozing drivers. Good research tells you a deodorant called No-Sweat might work in Australia, but probably nowhere else.

Good research leads you to the understanding that non-alcoholic lagers before the launch of Kaliber were regarded as a joke by beer drinkers. Once you've got that point you may have a springboard from which to go somewhere rather interesting .. . like, for instance, a serious, non-joking Billy Connolly and a great strapline.

Kaliber. Brewed by Guinness. No alcohol. No joke.

our mission is brilliance not mediocrity

But our mission is brilliance not mediocrity, which is why I want to focus on some easy-to-set-up research techniques which can lead you personally to eureka! moments. As Warren Buffett said:

'In the end I always believe my own eyes rather than something else.'

- **Online questionnaires**

  Done reasonably well these may tell you some of the real questions you should be asking. They are relatively cheap to administer and once you have a reasonable sample of respondents you can get very fast responses to questions you have.

- **Consumer complaint chatrooms**

  Robert Heller, the management guru, said his dilemma was that only one person in ten who had a complaint actually bothered to complain. He talked about soliciting complaints, because once you got them out in the open you could turn a critic into a fan by doing the sorry-I'll-put-this-right-now-and reward-you-for-your-patience performance.

- **Brand surgeries**

  Brand surgeries come from the world of politics and are how you, the brand steward, gets to meet your customers (your voters) and test out the temperature every now and again.

- **Super-groups**

  Consumer councils of reasonably expert people whom you can divide into simple classifications: people who will try anything that's new and interesting – in other words early adopters; those who are pragmatic and shop on price. But by far the most important group will be those most loyal to you because if ever you alienate this group you are in terrible and, probably, unnecessary trouble.

● **Consumer consultant pyramids**

In the first instance, these will typically be heavy users of whatever broad product category interests you, and well capable of enrolling a bunch of their friends to tell them what they think is going on. You can use these as eyes and ears in the marketplace or as a mechanic for running quick, low-key focus groups. Six such well-briefed and paid consultants may allow you to branch out to over 40 respondents.

● **What's new pussycat?**

This is about having a bunch of bright 'vigilantes' (vigilant people in the sense I want to use this word) who just in the course of their normal lives keep their eyes open for exciting innovations and inventions. The Dutch Innovation-Watchers called Trendwatching (the B2C division) and their B2B division, Springwise, have 8,000 trendspotters, so use them as your global telescope but build your own small army too, focusing on your business sector as well as being alive to general developments.

Caveat! Caveat! Caveat!

Do not live on a diet of DIY research alone. I am an opponent of pretty well DIY anything. But I believe passionately that to be brilliant at marketing you have to understand the rhythm of thinking and the patterns of behaviour of your consumers. The more you know about them and the more you empathise with them the better. Besides anything else, if you have your amateur groups of respondents who feed you ideas and attitudes then, when you decide you have to do a major, solid and as far as your board is concerned, credible, study from a well-known company, you will be able to give the research company the most magnificent brief because you'll already be halfway there.

Choosing brilliant research companies

● You will respect and be stimulated by what they say and the way they say it. If they are boring, however good their reputation, don't hire them.

● You want the best brains. How smart are they? Only the best will help you be brilliant and they MUST be great at speaking in a simple, easy-to-understand language.

● They will bring insights to what you are doing that provide exceptional value.

● They will have track records in your area so they can benchmark their observations against competition.

● They will be passionate about doing a brilliant job for you, providing something a bit extra. If they find this too difficult a challenge don't use them.

● Ask to see them at work before you hire them. Everyone has a right to test-drive an expensive sports car, which is what they are.

● Avoid big and boring. Contact www.theresearchbuyers guide.com to find out who's doing good stuff right now.

On commitment-driven marketing

Butch Rice and Jan Hofmeyer are both residents of South Africa and launched their 'Conversion Model™' around the world in 1986. In a world of many business and marketing books I happened on this book, *Commitment-Led Marketing*, that they wrote and liked it a lot. Here's what they say:

'At the high end of commitment, committed consumers act as advocates for the brand exhorting others to use it. In effect the more committed consumers you have the more effective your marketing efforts will be.'

Of course we intuitively know this. Just as we know our best friends are our most important friends. Yet in an age of networking we tend to try and extend our relationships even at the expense of those who trust and love us most.

'We define wastage as the expenditure of marketing funds on consumers who are unlikely to switch to the brand in the near term.'

This is the most key message of all brilliant marketing: focus on those people most likely to say 'yes'.

focus on those people most likely to say 'yes'.

But also recognise that when economic pressure prevails, a marketing volcano can follow. People who'd been loyal to Waitrose to the point of fisticuffs if anyone criticised them at a supper party slink off to Lidl when the going gets tough. M&S suits make way for the Aldi £25 suit. The new marketing message is often dictated by the times in which we live. Commitment can be 'wallet deep'.

'The more important a relationship is to a person the more willing the person will be to tolerate dissatisfaction in favour of trying to fix it.'

Look after your best customers. When involvement is low, the strength of a relationship cannot be that strong; when involvement is high, the consumers' strategy is to try and fix things when they go wrong. You really want to have a lot of 'best friends'.

 **example**

Dissimulation

Lamp-posts and babies

Butch Rice played a game whereby he produced a graph showing the relationship between the number of babies born and the number of lamp-posts in the world. He sought to show (quite bogusly of course) that birth rate was lamp-post dependent. Whereas the number of lamp-posts actually indicates density of population. One the best examples of ludicrous correlations you could find. This is an excellent example of lies, damned lies and statistics.

Learning

Tipping points

In getting people to support a charity there are three rules. One, you must ask and ask and ask. Two, you must be pleasant and clear. Three, you must make it easy to respond. In the recently published *Yes!* by Goldstein, Martin and Cialdini, they described how they'd researched the difference between asking for a donation for the American Cancer Society with and without this line – 'even a penny would help'. Donations with that line were 50 per cent, without it 29 per cent. QED: the case for using research well.

Summary

Research is a vital tool in brilliant marketing, but it is a chisel and sometimes your brilliance has been to create a beautiful marketing mahogany table. Be careful how you use one on the other.

(i) **Research has drawbacks**. It works on what has happened in the past – it is poor at trying to see the future and the really big things like life, death, fire and wheels.

(ii) **Only use the best researchers**. Too much work is done by low-grade moderators working with respondents who are groupies, spending most of their lives in sitting rooms in group discussions. Ask yourself if you'd trust these people to tell you how to run your life. Do their opinions hold more validity than your own?

(iii) ***Research is a radar system***. *Good research can provide you with great insights – look out for the insights not the whole truth.*

(iv) **Use your own ears and eyes too**. Make sure you have your own conduits to consumers. You cannot be a brilliant marketer unless you have a direct line to enough people who use and understand your brand.

(v) **Are your key customers committed to your brand?** The key in building a brilliant brand is to build as many people as you can who are really committed to it, not just loyal but who actually adore it.

Real brilliance comes from a passionate interest in people and a desire to know how they tick. It also comes from the realisation that people change their minds, their habits and nearly 40 per cent of them their partners.

Nothing in life stays the same for ever, least of all the attitudes and behaviour of those who matter most to us. Our consumers.

CHAPTER 26

As of today, everything's in play

Brilliant opportunities

Marketing is about changing things, about rearranging the cards you have in your hand. In the stable, stodgy 1960s when nothing much happened, brand shares changed slowly, marketing directors kept their jobs for ages and the sun shone in summer.

But in a new world where hurricanes destroy cities on a regular basis, where terrorism is a certainty, where catastrophe is a normal word, where companies get taken over or go bust constantly, where people keep on changing their minds, losing their jobs and where literally anything could happen, there has never been more opportunity for marketers.

But a new and a more brilliant kind of marketer.

The marketer of tomorrow will be more nimble, smarter and more inclined to experiment. In marketing we shall not be formulaic, but we shall try new things. Most of all we shall have to be creative and seek to engage not just the attention but also the imagination of the consumer.

> the marketer of tomorrow will be more inclined to experiment

There are four key questions.

(i)   **Exploitation**. How can we mobilise the mood of the moment so as to make the money we spend go further?

(ii) **Differentiation**. How can we stand out from the other marketers?

(iii) **Communication**. How can we establish a rapport with the consumer whereby we can build the kind of relationship with them whereby we can actually sell them something?

(iv) **Justification**. How can we prove to all those around us – especially our CFO – that we are providing a great, no better than that, a brilliant return on investment?

What is really going on?

If you wrote down what happened during 2007 and 2008 your very sensible editor would probably send it back to you with a note saying, 'Don't be silly – your readers aren't credulous idiots you know.'

In these strangely turbulent times almost anything can happen and probably will happen. It's expecting too much to achieve the state of nirvana to which Tom Peters so often refers – he called one of his books *Thriving on Chaos*.

brilliant tip

General Shinseki, a former US general, said:

'If you don't like change you're going to like irrelevance even less.'

Change everything now

We live in a world where new replaces old, decentralised replaces bureaucratic, fast replaces slow, small replaces big, light replaces heavy, smart replaces predictable, information replaces weight of personnel, open replaces control and command. But there's more to it all than this.

The absolute absence of certainty, stability and long-term clarity of vision will impact on all we do and not least on marketing. The elements of change infect everything. And a new word worse than 'infect' invaded our vocabulary in 2008 – it was 'corrode'. It's start again time.

> the absolute absence of certainty will impact on all we do and not least on marketing

Nude shock horror

Here are the kind of things that we have discovered in a world where the Emperor was not only discovered to be naked but so too was all his court and, indeed, where, to be blunt, clothing seemed to be something of a rarity. As Warren Buffett said, 'When the tide goes out you see who's been swimming naked.' In the twenty-first century it would appear that skinny-dipping was the norm.

New rules of life and marketing

- Those who control the money control everything. The banks, the major retailers, the venture capitalists, governments.

- In a global economy it is impossible to predict the effect of local action – if government A does something ostensibly sensible and traders in countries B and C decide to block it, they probably can. Everything is immediate in today's open-media world.

- You are only as good as what you did last.

- People have discovered they can and must change their minds. John Maynard Keynes rather tartly responded to the accusation that he had changed his mind again with this:

'When circumstances change I change my mind – what do you do?'

- – unspoken but clearly embedded – *you stupid, unthinking lemming.*

- No one is impervious to disaster however big and rich they are.

- People only deserve the respect that their actions create – title is meaningless as are background, education and reputation.

- There is a rhythm of life that we have sacrificed for cash and some people in the future will revert to the 'good life'.

- Only talk about strategy when you have a child beside you, because it's only in their presence you have a real feel for the real future, their future.

- The age of the mean-spirited bastard is over – sorry, chaps, you are history. Management has to work in an increasingly decentralised world where the customer has the power to say 'no'.

- Innovation, when it happens, will produce things that are better, faster and cheaper, like the Dyson Airblade, like Gillette Mach 3, like digital radio, like broadband.

- We are going to spend the rest of our marketing lives worrying about relationships and realise that it is the relationship between a brand and its customers that matters – nothing else.

- Anything that interrupts that relationship is in peril. Hence the growth in direct insurance and e-commerce practitioners like Amazon.

- The only way of measuring marketing brilliance will be in assessing the strength and the level of commitment (on both sides) in this relationship.

- What Charles Darwin actually said was not that 'the fittest survive' but this, which was much more to the point:

'In the struggle for survival, the fittest win out at the expense of their rivals because they succeed in adapting themselves best to their environment.'

Marketers have got to be much more adaptable.

- Two choices about choice:

  i)   the stress of too much choice is going to come under major review. The big retailers are going to cut back on stock-keeping units because it's both an unsustainable business model and has created a paranoid consumer base – too much cacophony, too many second-rate options. We are going to ask this question, all of us, 'Can we improve our lives by getting rid of what is irrelevant?'

  ii)   or, more likely, choice will grow, e-commerce will grow, multiple choice and customisation will take place on the web. It's hard to turn back the clock, and genuine innovation is what drives the marketing machine and the interest of media and customer alike.

So long as marginal improvements can be made 'new improved' will be better than 'same-as'.

What price premium pricing?

The debate about pricing goes on and on and not least between Stephen Martin, who owns Market Clarity who focuses on B2B and mainly on high tech, and me. He is a bold-pricer. I am a cautious-pricer, which means I think pricing is at the epicentre of current marketing, whereas he doesn't really think pricing is the major factor.

Well, to be fair, that was before the economic hurricane started blowing in 2007 and 2008. Then all bets were off.

I have seen this Aldi, Netto, Lidl resurgence thing coming for some time. But it's suddenly become a middle-class storm – a word-of-mouth hurricane.

The modern consumer everywhere except the UK has become used to low price retail and cheap cars. The UK was once called 'Treasure Island' by the motor trade and where else in the EU are grocers getting the margins Tesco and Sainsbury's get? Price has been used as a 'trumpeted rather than delivered' marketing tool until mid-2008 when the 'hey that's cheap' Lidls of this world hit the scene.

From aggregators in insurance to Aldi for suits at £25, to Asda where you get a serviceable white shirt for £3 and a pair of socks for 30p, price has become the increasing discriminator. Primark is a power brand now complementing the handbags of Prada. While Muji is a great and fabulously cheap, Japanese brand with a concise range of beautifully designed items for flats and home offices. And everywhere everyone has a sale on – the whole time – even before Christmas.

So what's going on here?

If you have a brand you may be able to survive price cutting longer than most – if it's a really strong brand. BA loses out to the rottweilers at a budget airline – 'And did we say you could smile? Shut up, you vile customers. Stop whining. You make us so sick with your puerile expectations of customer service.' And Innocent loses out to homemade smoothies. And the best-selling wine in the USA – [yellow tail] – is the price-promoting brand.

Watch out you solid, safe bets

In the first decade of the twenty-first century price is going to become more important as we move from a want-based buying culture to a needs-based one.

- Watch out for private educational establishments doing price promotions, with radical cost-cutting and bank-rolling customers because they'll be under real pressure.

- Watch car showrooms where salesmen will sweat as their customers sweetly force down the price and where for once female customers will be treated beautifully.

- Watch bank managers squirm as they pitch and repitch for business.

- Watch everyone learning to negotiate – nothing will be at face value. Someone I know always demands and gets a farmers' discount – and he's not a farmer. Never buy anything without asking for a discount – a 'bottom-friendly' as they seem to call it in the antique trade.

- You win a contract – open the champagne – and then watch the procurement team enter the room to negotiate the final terms. They make undertakers look like the life and soul of the party. Put the champagne away. You may not want the contract by the time they've finished with you.

As far as the consumer is concerned tomorrow belongs to them. And they will have just a few things to say to the retailer and brand owner:

> as far as the consumer is concerned tomorrow belongs to them

- Q. How much? **TOO MUCH**.
- Q. How long to deliver? **TOO LONG**.
- Q. How good? **NOT GOOD ENOUGH. UPGRADE, PLEASE**.

Premium quality at discount price is here for the next decade or so. Get used to it – they have in the USA. And as marketers you will get used to it, if you are going to be brilliant as opposed to having your head stuck in sand.

brilliant tip

There will be two sorts of marketers in the future: ostriches and
meerkats. Having your head in the sand or being ever vigilant. Do
not suppose the old rules apply any more. They don't.

Some changes in today's marketing world

Keep on trying to work out what's changing, what's the same
and how these changes impact on what you are doing and how
you can take advantage of them. Here are just a few trends.

- **My castle, not my pension**

  As the relationship fundamentally changes between people
  and their homes we can expect more redecorating, more
  nesting, more gardening and more 'staycations' – that's
  holidaying at home.

- **New 'me-ism'**

  Dr Phil on the *Larry King Show* during the American
  Primaries in 2008 spoke about when people ask that
  poleaxe question *'what's in it for me?'* when considering a
  candidate's credentials. The agenda has changed – global
  warming and being kind to animals is slipping down the
  agenda, the pound in my pocket and my children's welfare
  is moving up the agenda.

- **Niches splinter again and again – sawdust everywhere**

  Mass marketing RIP. Which is sad if you want an easy life.
  But to achieve brilliance we have to be patient and
  understand that mass is a mess and that niche is nice. Local
  issues are becoming more important and global issues
  harder to comprehend. Short-term political pressures will
  drive the former.

- **Branding crazy**

  Brand used to be a word only used by marketers. Now everyone uses it. Politicians. Bankers. Bishops. The penny dropped or rather the million-pound realisation hit people when they realised brands were worth money.

- **That urgent need to be famous and popular**

  From *Big Brother* to the Mr Bean habit of sending yourself birthday cards there is an obsession about being seen to be popular and famous. If you're under 30 and you aren't in the news or on TV or talked about you are a loser. We live in an age of 'star-seekers'. It will affect the way we do marketing.

- **Fantasy consumers, fantasy marketing**

  This comprises using actors as consumers and generally just making things up; PR people sending in favourable reviews to chatrooms, all that kind of thing. Bottom line – be very circumspect when you come across a piece of research because it could have been made up. Beware consumer testimonials. Almost everything nowadays needs a health warning to be attached to it.

- **Bogus authenticity**

  We see an increasing need to have craftsmanship on the front of an item and evidence of items ageing – brand old as opposed to brand new is cool. Second hand is on the way back. This especially applies to watches. And how about this from Danny Pizzigoni of Royal Arcade Watches, Burlington Arcade:

  'The most sought-after vintage watches are those that were unpopular at the time they were first on sale because fewer were made.'

- **Naughty but nice**

  Not a new trend this – there used to be a dining club in advertising called 'the Fat Boys' Club', but we may see a reversion to smoking, drinking bitter and eating suet-based, high-calorie meals especially among a rebellious niche particularly of men fed up with the strait-laced diet-obsessed world of today.

- **Miss Goody two shoes**

This is exactly the opposite (just to make things more confusing); nothing bad for you at all. Size zero; lemon and boiling water; pilates; yoga; broccoli soup; colonic irrigation; young ladies who shrink (and young men as well). *'I feel and look wonderful'*, she squealed and then she fainted.

- **Gossip, rumours and realities**

Rumours are the new marketing tool. It's what made shorting shares so potent a way of making money – otherwise known as 'trash and cash'. Anything goes in the super-fast era in which we live, even lies. But the reality is we all gossip and spread stories, not just the paparazzi and the *Sun*. The trend to gossip has exploded, aided by the web and social networking.

- **A new language has been born**

It's gr8 2 c. No, it's gone beyond texting; it's 'Kwikspeke'. When educational academics actually recommend that we abandon spelling, as we know it, because it's too difficult and is inhibiting learning we need to watch out. Abbreviations and acronyms are the thing now. Hence BoJo (Boris Johnson); BoMo (Bournemouth); LMAO – work it out or rather WIO. Shakespeare introduced over 2,000 new words. Expect a volley of new language . . . it goes with globalisation.

- **The little things mean a lot**

In marketing you need points of difference and interesting points of detail to talk about, not just unique selling propositions. In Shine Communication's book *Embrace the Chaos*, they call this 'The Cupholder Principle' – viz. it's the principle of making major purchasing decisions on the basis of small details like the cupholder in a BMW.

- **Today, winning is all that matters**

  We used to enjoy playing the game, then we all got prizes win or lose, now the need to win seems all absorbing. It's what drives *Big Brother* and its sibling shows, it's what drives the success of *Strictly Come Dancing* (and wait for the variants which will follow that – *Strictly Come Cooking, Strictly Come Running* and so on).

- **Nothing is impossible**

  This was the Saatchi & Saatchi mantra of the 1980s. They were right. Jaguar is owned by the Indian company Tata. Aston Martin is jointly owned by Kuwait and British investors. Smoking is banned in pubs and restaurants – if you'd told anyone that in 1988 they'd have said you were crazy. Do not be conservative – the world is too turbulent for that. Think of the impossible – bet you it happens. '*Your flight PIG 1 is now boarding at Gate 8*' – see I told you.

Conclusion

It may seem a little frightening to state everything's in play, but no more frightening than the fact we are all going to die one day. What it suggests is we are going to have to be cleverer and faster and that brilliant marketing will be demanded by shareholders.

It's a big challenge but it might be a lot of fun; brilliant fun in fact.

PART 5

A summary and highlights

Why marketing matters

Marketing has never been more important because business has never been so competitive.

Learn how to do it, how to be knowledgeable about where it's changing and why it's changing and what drives change. Most of all learn how to understand the customer and their new found power.

CHAPTER 27

Summary and highlights

What is this 'brilliant marketing' thing?

I t's about the art of seducing the customer. This is more art than science. It's about raising that bar because less than A* is a fail. This is

brilliance in marketing comes from awareness

exciting stuff. It's about mindsets and skillsets as well as something we really need – smartsets – the ability to speak to the street not to a boardroom. Brilliance in marketing comes from awareness and from creativity not from formulae.

Let's get marketing into context. The psychology, history and alchemy of marketing

Brilliant marketing is best learned from the best people and is about balancing left and right brain so we are acutely keen on gauging performance, fanatic about measurement and money, as well as developing a wonderful sense of intuition. But marketing is a discipline based around 'return on investment' too, which you must learn. The world is changing. We have to work in close-knit and high-performance teams and apply a rigour of questioning that makes accountancy look like pretty ordinary, basic arithmetic. Key questions on context are as follows:

Have you got the right stuff to be marketer?

Look in the mirror. Find that energy and creativity; you must decide if you want to get by, to get on or to go places. Learn how to change your mindset because in a very unpredictable and competitive world you dare not be predictable any more than a bridge player dare be an 'easy-read'. Do you love selling? You'd better love it – it's at the core of your life. Are you an optimist? Be one who espouses the mantra 'anything is possible'. And do you like people? Because marketing is about human beings and through skill, charm and deft communication getting them to do what otherwise they wouldn't do.

Do you understand the history of marketing, past and present and have you a feel for the future?

Ninety per cent of the major brands are much older than you. But the world is changing very fast. The facts of life are that being good at marketing has got a lot harder. But understand the six ages of marketing and you can hold your own with anyone; from the first TV ad, in 1955, to the two-word-equity, integrated campaigns of today. We are witnessing the end of mass marketing and the emergence of something more intimate and conversational. And we have to understand that customers simply don't have enough time nowadays. Customers are in charge; marketing-speak is dead; as is noisy. The world demands leaders not marketers, which is what the modern marketer has to be. There's never been a more important time to be in marketing.

Do you understand how brands and brilliance work?

What is a brand in simple, meaningful words? Nike is an example of a brilliantly created and developed brand. The key lesson is to never, ever be boring. And it's about understanding that a brand is a man-made artefact with some 'clever' triggers that simply induces people to pay more for it. A brand is a product with a personality about which consumers have feelings, not just thoughts. It is something remembered and trusted. We can help you make a brand. In return you must promise not to preach to customers, but to let the brand develop and grow with their help and input. Living proof of brand power is the Coca-Cola New Coke fiasco. The customer will always fight back.

Do you understand what marketing tools you need? We invite you, ladies and gentlemen, to choose your weapons

There is a journey of discovery around the different marketing techniques and just how they can be made to work best and most economically.

I don't recommend DIY marketing but believe you need to know how to cope with the 'experts' by really understanding the language of marketing and how the tools work and by being competent at DIY if you have no other choice.

Advertising – the root of the great sales pitch

Is advertising dying? The art of story-telling is at the centre of all marketing and sales. Hip-swaggering advertising still works because it's the soul of selling. In a world where ideas are vital, this is the factory from which many of the best will come. To become versed in the art will take a lot of time and mean looking at a lot of advertising. Look at the best on YouTube and as you do so, remember this is an art not a formula and that fresh and original will have the sharpest cut-through. Remember also that if an idea makes you laugh it's a sure sign it's a good idea.

> the art of story-telling is at the centre of all marketing and sales

How to make advertising work

First, get the message right, and to learn how to do this spend as long as it takes working out how you are superior to the competition and what the customer really thinks, feels and believes about you; and only lead with one idea because the customer can only catch one ball at a time. Be obsessive about being on brief, being engaging and asking if this will make any difference to the way people behave. Have a foolproof checklist. Get your agencies to deliver by treating them well and making them value your business not just for the money. Think like an ad man by being interested in advertising and what it does to people. Develop eclectic tastes in music, film and literature.

All about media

You need to show your advertising where it will reach the people you want to reach. You need to understand the different kinds of media and how they work. If you have a small budget for a local brand, examine the magic of radio, posters and local press used in conjunction. Look at specialist magazines to maximise the accuracy of your targeting. Media is changing. It's harder and more expensive to reach big audiences. Newspapers are making off to the web. The key to planning a media schedule is your budget and your key objectives. This is a difficult area, so I believe you should be briefing the experts, especially when it comes to buying. Avoid making your media too complicated.

PR – just give them the facts

PR is about solid fact-based stories, it is not about lies and spin. It's also about preserving the most important corporate and brand asset of all – reputation.

Learning how to face the media in interviews takes training. Do not assume it is easy; even the experts like politicians struggle to get it right. If you want a story to run in the media, make sure you have an interesting angle. Journalists hate sales blurbs and love stories with edge. PR has moved from champagne bars (pity that!) and the sidelines to being a key marketing component. Lots of techniques are available to help make companies seem more important and interesting. PR has become the champion of thought leadership. Great PR people have a great sense of zeitgeist.

Sponsorship or living close to excitement

Unless you can invest properly and spend time bringing your sponsorship to life, this can be a dodgy investment. As a rule of thumb, whatever it costs you to secure the sponsorship should be doubled to give you an adequate exploitation budget. Due diligence and a long list of questions is needed; and, most importantly, can you get the time and devotion of the team or individuals you are sponsoring and can you justify it in terms of return on investment? Can you make news with the sponsorship? Can it secure you an advantage with your channels of distribution? Sponsorship is often entered into for poor reasons, but if it fits and says big things about your brand it can be fabulous and impressive.

Design is it!

Design is a crucial differentiator, whether it be in the product itself or its packaging. You can fall in love with brilliant design and that's just what consumers do. Look at the response Steve Jobs got when he introduced new and brilliantly designed products from Apple. Design can win sales much faster than hype. Great design starts with a great design brief and with deep thinking about what you want to achieve. Consider the power of a John Deere or of Stanley tools; consider that DreamWorks logo; relish Dyson for look and functionality. Great design lies at the heart of great branding – see what the Heinz packaging with what they call the Heinz keystone – that framing device – achieves. I ♥ design.

Direct marketing is about money and measuring results

Direct marketing lives in the world of conversations – face-to-face, by letter, by phone or by email; the world of precise targeting; the world of instant measurement; the world of building customer relationships; the world of sales. As marketing has moved from mass to segmented to niche marketing DM has found a key role, especially in direct sales situations like direct insurance, online banking and e-commerce. Understanding how to build, develop and care for a database is key – that's what makes the work Dunhumby has done for Tesco so impressive. Yet there's room for improvement as so much of the DM material is frankly a bit dull. When creativity and mathematics embrace we'll have an interesting explosion of wealth.

Customer relationship marketing – the experience

We live in a service economy. In service, first impressions are critical – that's why a great reception and brilliant receptionist are so important. It's where the love affair with your customers starts. So learning how to serve brilliantly is critical. Choosing the right people so they live and champion your brand values is a start. Then learning to smile and engage with your customers is next. Have a smiling mouth and listening ears. You are the brand – live its values. Be a brand warrior, not a pathetic brand wimp who doesn't care about the brand they work for. Be a brand warrior who'd fight to keep and please their customers and remember 'the customer's right even when they are wrong'. Always.

Experiential marketing – the experience in wide screen and technicolour

The science of the senses can be used to predispose people to buy. Thus the sound of birdsong has been proven to increase sales, the smell of coffee sells houses and the smell of baking bread sells more groceries. This takes service to an entirely new and dramatic level. Use all the senses to seduce the consumer. Imagine a 'total experience' dome – it'll happen soon. All experience currently says people want the real thing, which is live performance. See it in retail at Selfridges, see it on stage at the O2 arena. Use the senses to sell.

Buzz marketing is when they all start talking about you

This is the category of ambient, event and word of mouth marketing. It involves happenings, theatre and the unexpected. It's about learning to be a rebel and recognising that what we used to do doesn't work because the consumer is boss and is answering back to marketing corporations. From Ben & Jerry's sampling parties to doing street advertising for a vegetarian restaurant chain using a sweet calf, to sculpting a car in ice to doing a tightrope walk at 10,000 feet – all are events that get people talking. Do something like this and watch momentum build. Fun stuff.

Digital marketing and why the future will never be the same

When commercial TV started in 1955 the impact on marketing was similar to the effect digital is having today. Now more money is spent on the web than on TV advertising. So beware! I love the thought that through your mobile phone we know where you are and can direct you to the nearest whatever it is you want. I love the diversity, creativity and impact of web sites. I love viral ads. I love the fact that the answer to the question, 'Who is CEO of the internet?' is a snort and a guffaw. I love the absence of command and control. Seth Godin tells us about ordinary conversations and what he calls 'permission marketing'. Social utilities like Facebook and MySpace between them reach over 360 million users. Big numbers. It is the openness and propensity to change that is so appealing, with handsets becoming the weapon of choice. Just check out the remorseless growth of shopping online and the explosion in technology through at last fast broadband. The new world of marketing is young and exciting.

Branded entertainment and other revolutions

Big brands are investing in, and acting in effect as sponsors, for film, TV series and theatre. The smartest want content control – hence *Pot Noodle: The Musical* at the 2008 Edinburgh Fringe, hence the novel by Fay Weldon, *The Bulgari Connection*. This is about a brand take-over whereby the patrons of the arts and other events may be Coca-Cola, Procter & Gamble and Apple. And this is just one of the new marketing techniques; from laser shows on to clouds – brands owning the skies – to 'fake' events like mixing theatre and cinema with the audience having actor plants among them, to painting a town pink – which is what Mattel did for Barbie. There are no limits to brand imagination today.

The nitty-gritty part of the marketing story is in creating and executing a great marketing plan

And this isn't easy. When you contemplate the depth of questioning and the amount of work needed to validate hypotheses, whether that be through research, workshops, studying competitive marketing plans, pulling products apart to see what truly stands up to the rigours of today's world, or lengthy financial analyses with your colleagues in finance, marketing is now a long way apart from its superficially creative phase when marketers were rumoured to be moody and Byronic, saying things like 'let's do something different; let's paint it green'. Marketing is an art underpinned by the most robust and demanding factual and scientific, forensic analytical work.

The first steps in creating a marketing campaign

You have to write a compelling and exciting marketing brief – even if you have a one-person business, doing this will force you to think about what you want to achieve and what your limitations, realistically, are. To write a decent brief find a simple template (I've given you two of these – the brief brief and the longer brief). Focus on who you want to talk to, what you want to say and what you want them to do; this will be a complex and brain-aching exercise. Define your budget – how much can you afford and what return over what period are you seeking? Now it's time to choose your marketing weapons and how much of each you need/can afford. Final piece of advice. Excite yourself because it's showtime!

Refining objectives, messages and mood

The marketing process isn't mechanical but is an iterative process where just because you've written a brief doesn't mean to say you can't improve it. You need to reassess objectives, debate messages, see how to sharpen them and how to tell them even more vividly. You are looking to do things in tandem. Create a big, compelling, colourful story and make sure all the details work too; a combination of big sweep and intricate. Just never get complacent.

How to write a brilliant marketing plan

Having done the preparatory work it's time to write it down and be judged by your bosses and peers. Great plans need to be meticulously planned. First of all regard them as plans for success. Ultimately they are selling documents, asking for investment funding, and if successful at achieving that end then act as a cross between a Bible and a very detailed route map. First of all, understand that a strategy is a clearly defined destination and everything else falls into place. Second, know the key headings for any half-decent marketing plan:

● Executive summary
● Corporate background
● Brand/product/service – detailed evaluation
● Key customer targets

- History of the brand
- Current brand status
- Comparative analysis versus all competition – key issues
  - Product
  - Customers
  - Distribution channel
  - Pricing
  - Marketing
  - Sales
  - Human capital
  - Green and ethical issues
- Key objectives
- Marketing strategy and strategic plan
- Current and future customer targets
- Opportunities and challenges
- Resource analysis
- Strategic and tactical milestones in fulfilling the plan
- Detailed business plan and financials
- How (in detail) will the plan be delivered
  - strategic plans by each category
  - activity map by item
  - sell-in plan
- Team credentials
- Appendices

Make the plan look professional and carefully put together but not flashy. Use plenty of visuals. Make sure you have a PowerPoint summary presentation ready to use. Good luck. Just keep it strong and simple.

How to choose and manage suppliers, agencies and brilliant people

You have to cast the dream team, people who rock, because in the end it is people who make the key difference. Talent in the flesh always beats talent on paper. Seek a series of first impressions by meeting anyone you might be going to work with several times. Take a lot of trouble and time finding and then choosing professional advisers. If you choose someone without having felt the chemistry of working with them happen, you are foolish. Learn how to inspire, energise and direct people around you and your agencies. The magic cocktail lies in just four words 'well done' and 'thank you' and remember people who like you will try harder for you.

Managing the marketing campaign

Now you have that plan, turn it into a successful reality. Become an execution machine. How? You need to champion it. Make sure that the detailed implementation is on track on a daily basis. That debate, and from different points of view, is encouraged. That you keep a paper trail of everything that happens. That you get out into the marketplace on a regular basis. That you are happy to change anything (or anyone) that isn't working – quickly. That you have fast, detailed and comprehensive feedback from the market the whole time. Don't guess. That the team is well co-ordinated and aligned. That you applaud learning from failure and that you celebrate success. That you support, love and grow with your team. This is very big job to get right. Throw yourself into it.

Sorry. There's been a budget cut

That's life and it's going to happen. Don't grumble. Sort it. Avoid waste . . . get things right first time. The amount of money wasted through spurious or theatrical perfectionism is criminal. When you construct your plan do a hidden Plan B, C and D which envisage a cut of 10 per cent, 20 per cent, 30 per cent, so you at least can respond to a crisis with a thought-through response. Check and recheck the anticipated return on investment of each component in the plan – if any one of them is delivering below par put pressure on to adjust the cost or prepare to ditch it. See if you can buy better – this will apply to agency remuneration – or can they do more for the same? In today's climate all costs are negotiable. Look at people overheads – if you could increase the amount done per hour by ⅙, and extend the working day by an hour, you should be able to do the same amount of work with around 25 per cent fewer people. Look at using freelancers to handle variable work. Avoid fixed costs if you can. Simplify the plan. Attack fewer targets in a smaller geography. And of course in the first place, if you're smart, you'll have built in a contingency. Saving cost is par for the business world nowadays. Just do it.

Sophisticated techniques and concepts come into play when you have to talk strategy, creativity and the bigger picture. To be part of the future you have to be change-responsive and forward-looking

This stuff about creativity, the mind games they call strategy, the many research techniques that make psychologists salivate and the art of futurology are all part of the toolkit a modern marketer needs to have, if not at their fingertips then, at least in their mind. This is a sophisticated profession – here are some of the more exotic aspects of it.

Creativity and ways to turn brilliance into reality

You think you can't be creative? Think again. There are techniques which will change the way you approach creativity and the way you do marketing for ever. Being creative is having the ability to make unusual connections and cross-reference ideas.

It's about being relaxed enough to have lots of ideas. It's about inspiring people so you change their minds. And that's the most creative thing you can do. You start by having a vivid curiosity. You are very people focused. You think about creative things and really think about how they work. You travel; you look; you listen. You work in teams just kicking ideas around. You create a crisis (don't bother – one will have just happened anyway) – how do you solve it? Amazing how a group of you will find unusual creative solutions. Go out and talk to your customers. Listen to your inner voice. Let your subconscious work – let ideas stew for a while. Let's go for it. We used to be the most inventive nation in the world. Let's get there again by applying that nascent talent to design, new products and marketing instead of financial instruments.

Running a marketing workshop

Workshops allow teams to unleash their talent and their creativity. Workshops sharpen competitive instincts. Activities vary from creating mood boards to acting out what the competitors might do by debating and challenging key issues. To make workshops really work you need a great facilitator. The process involves the following elements: introduction, investigation, complication, creation, focus, development, alignment. This isn't random – it's a process that works. Quality of preparation and clarity of purpose will impact on quality of output.

Market research. Are these rude words?

Research can kill good ideas or give you wonderful insights. You need to find out how to get the latter consistently and really understand and develop a 'feel' for your customer. But research is only a guide. Dame Anita Roddick said, 'Using research to manage a business is like using the rear-view mirror to drive a car.' It is unlikely that fire or the wheel would have survived focus groups with cavemen, as the Idea Group in San Diego entertainingly shows. The types of research to choose from are bafflingly wide but I espouse getting among customers and asking some pretty direct questions through online questionnaires, chatrooms, surgeries, super-groups with early adopter customers, customer consultants and vigilantes (ordinary people you appoint as 'lookouts'). In short, keep your own personal radar system well tuned. And yes, of course use professional research but don't lose the skill of being a 'listening post' yourself. When you use pros, use ones who inspire you and can give you deep insight into your competitors. Overall, focus most of your early attention on your most loyal and committed customers . . . any sign of unrest there is an early warning signal of trouble. Any signs of this cohort growing is just the reverse. So research is good and helpful when used as a torch rather than as a truncheon.

research is good and helpful when used as a torch rather than as a truncheon

Change and crisis. How everything's in play right now

Turmoil? Chaos? It's normal nowadays. In a global economy we'll continue to see it. Those with the skill to cope will win. And change and chaos will continue to lie at the heart of our marketing environment.

Conclusion

Marketing is more art than science but you need skills to succeed and techniques to make sound judgements. This book teaches you to have both.

CHAPTER 28

Read and see

Here are a few of the
things that have shaped
my marketing life. I don't
want you to be a geek but
I do want you to be
interested and observant.

Happy watching

Watch the highest rating programmes on TV; once a month go on a 'channel-hop' so you can see what's on the more obscure channels. Look at the best ads on YouTube. Watch www.adbrands.net.

Go out and buy a lot of magazines and flip through them, asking yourself – why are they designed like this?

Read the marketing news

- *Campaign*
- *Marketing*
- *Marketing Week*
- *Financial Times*
- *The Sun*
- *Sunday Times Style Magazine*
- *Creative Review*
- D&AD annuals

Read some of the best books on marketing and business

Those marked by an asterisk (or in rare cases two asterisks) are essential

General background

The Want Makers, Eric Clark

Key Marketing Skills, Peter Cheverton

Bright Marketing, Robert Craven

The New Marketing Manifesto, John Grant*

Kellogg on Marketing, edited by Dawn Iacobucci

Mastering Marketing Financial Times MBA Companion

Great Answers to Tough Marketing Questions, P.R. Smith

Advertising

The Advertiser's Manual, Stephen Baker

Behind the Scenes in Advertising, Jeremy Bullmore *

The Practice of Advertising, Normal Hart (Editor)

Great Advertising Campaigns, Nicholas Ind

Does it Pay to Advertise, John Philip Jones

The World's Best 100 Posters, Rob Morris and Richard Watson **

Confessions of an Advertising Man, David Ogilvy 1963 *

Ogilvy on Advertising, David Ogilvy 1983 **

Advertising Pure and Simple, Hank Seiden

What Advertising Is, Maurice Smelt * (Editor)

Brands

Brand Simple, Allen P. Adamson

Understanding Brands, Don Cowley (Editor)

Brand Warriors, Fiona Gilmore (Editor)

No Logo, Naomi Klein

Eating the Big Fish, Adam Morgan ★★

Brand Valuation, John Murphy (Editor)

Brand Storm, Will Murray

Brand Hijack, Alex Wibberfurth ★

Research and socio-economic background

The World is Flat, Thomas L. Friedman

Blink, Malcolm Gladwell ★

Qualitative Market Research, Wendy Gordon and Roy Langmaid

Commitment-Led Marketing, Jan Hofmeyr and Butch Rice ★★

Buyology, Martin Lindstrom

Why Men Don't listen and Women Can't Read Maps, Allan and
   Barbara Pease

Thriving on Chaos, Tom Peters

The Popcorn Report, Faith Popcorn ★

Direct Marketing

Common Sense Direct Marketing, Drayton Bird

Enterprise One to One, Don Peppers and Martha Rogers ★

The Great Marketing Turn-around, Stan Rapp and Thomas Collins

Maxi Marketing, Stan Rapp and Thomas Collins

Design

The Image of a Company, Introduced by Cees de Jong

A Smile in the Mind, Beryl McAlhone and David Stuart ★★

Brand New, Jane Pavitt (Editor) ★

Total Branding by Design, Paul Southgate

30 – Sedley Place's Anniversary Celebration, collated by Mick Nash and the Sedley Place team ★

Buzz marketing and digital

Improperganda – the Art of the Publicity Stunt, Mark Borowski ★

Permission Marketing, Seth Godin ★

Purple Cow, Seth Godin

Advertising is Dead . . . Long Live Advertising!, Tom Himpe ★★

Connected Marketing, Justin Kirby and Paul Marsden (Editors)

The Cluetrain Manifesto, Rick Levine, Christopher Locke, Doc Searls and David Weinberger ★★

Guerilla Marketing, Jay Conrad Levinson

Creativity

?Whatif! How to Start a Creative Revolution at Work, Dave Allan, Matt Kingdon, Kris Murrin and Daz Rudkin

It's Not How Good You Are, It's How Good You Want To Be, Paul Arden

Winnie-the-Pooh on Problem Solving, Roger and Stephen Allen

Serious Creativity, Edward de Bono

Yes! 50 Secrets from the Science of Persuasion, Noah Goldstein, Stephen Martin and Robert Cialdini

The Circle of Innovation, Tom Peters ★

Creativity in Business, Michael Ray and Rochelle Myers ★

Stuff every marketer ought to know about
The New Barbarian Manifesto, Ian Angell ★

The Starfish and the Spider, Ori Brafman and Rod Beckstrom ★★

The Great Reckoning, James Dale Davidson and William Rees-Mogg

The Rhythm of Life, Professor Russell Foster and Leon Kreitzman

The E-Myth Revisited, Michael Gerber ★

The Tipping Point, Malcolm Gladwell ★

The 24 Hour Society, Leon Kreitzman ★

What is Strategy and Does it Matter?, Richard Whittington

About great companies
The Rise and Fall of Marks and Spencer, Judi Bevan

Barbarians at the Gate, Bryan Burrough and John Helyar ★★

The Brothers, Ivan Fallon

The Wal-Mart Effect, Charles Fishman

The Nike Culture, Robert Goldman and Stephen Papson ★

Alpha Dogs, James Harding ★

The Google Story, David Vise

Jack, Jack Welch ★★

Managing different businesses

Good to Great, Jim Collins *

The Communication Catalyst, Mickey Connolly and Richard Rianoshek

Managing in the Service Economy, James L. Heskett

Managing Cultural Differences, Lisa Hoecklin *

The 'Nice' Company, Tom Lloyd

Re-Imagine!, Tom Peters *

On presenting and career development

Brilliant Presentation, Richard Hall

The Secrets of Success at Work, Richard Hall

Experience the marketing world at first hand and at low cost

Shops

Go from Selfridges to Primark; go from Whole Food Stores to Lidl; go from Daunts to Waterstone's in Piccadilly – and if you don't live in London go to the equivalent set of contrasts in say Leeds or York. Become a 'curious shopper'.

Cities in the UK

Go to Glasgow, Liverpool, Newcastle, Birmingham, London and Brighton and think about what's similar, what's different and what's surprising.

Countries

Now try somewhere you haven't been before in Europe (Berlin?) and Turkey (Ankara?) and the United States (Chicago?) and Africa (Pretoria?) and India (Nagpur?) and China (Chengdu?)

and South America (Sao Paolo?) New experiences that are out of the ordinary with rich stories to tell.

People

Meet the brightest and the best at a whole variety of events that are constantly being held at the RSA, the IOD, the Marketing Society, and organisations like WARC – who do great stuff . . .

WARC Conference Department
[mailto:mail.bniupjurvwddejm@marketing.warc.com]

Do not be shy about asking people what they think.

Sports

Go to watch a match – soccer, rugby, football and observe the whole tribal thing, which is quite brilliant and inspiring. And if you get the chance, do the same thing in the United States where everything is elevated to a new marketing experience.

The arts

Go and watch local art – music, theatre, whatever and for a few pounds (and often free) you'll experience great stuff. Stop going to show-stoppers at vast prices. Example: front row, six feet from Nicola Benedetti at a lunchtime Brighton concert cost £7.00. Start shopping.

Cathedrals

Go to Suffolk and look at churches like Long Melford – a cathedral in a village – once one of the richest churches in the world – memento mori – Lavenham, Southwold or the astonishing remnants of Bury St Edmunds (and check out *that* history). Or visit Canterbury, Winchester, Worcester, Ely, Salisbury and explore in your mind the wonders of ecclesiastical marketing. Now go to Canary Wharf, the City of London or Wall Street and see new forms of worship.

Transport

St Pancras, Terminal 5, Grand Central Station, Milan Station and go on the Shanghai Maglev or less excitingly the Bullet Train. Fly in a hot air balloon.

Markets

Go to Borough Market, Portobello or Petticoat Lane; visit the market at Chartres, or the market at Bayeux, in Italy try the Bologna food market. In Asia and South America go to any market you can find. Just enjoy the smells and the simple art of marketing. Look how they display things and talk about them.

Shopping centres

Visit Blue Water, Westfield, Meadowhall. And if you can, the South China Mall in Donguan, the Dubai Mall and the West Edmonton Mall in Canada.

Index